GREAT LIVES

Marie Antoinette

GREAT LIVES

Marie Antoinette

Annunziata Asquith

Introduction by Elizabeth Longford

Book Club Associates London

ISB 0 297 76766·6

House editor Jenny Ashby
Art editor Andrew Shoolbred
Layout by Margaret Fraser

Filmset and printed Offset Litho in Great Britain by
Cox & Wyman Ltd, London, Fakenham and Reading

Contents

Introduction

No HEROINE OF HISTORY OR FICTION has captured the imagination of posterity more completely than Marie Antoinette. Though numbing pathos rather than high tragedy is the dominant note, her story is unsurpassed. No doubt a Cathy of *Wuthering Heights* or an Anna Karenina will stir us more profoundly by a depth and richness of character which the unhappy French Queen did not possess, at least in youth. Marie Antoinette seems at first sight superficial. Ill-educated and 'giddy' according to her own mother the Empress Maria Theresa, she had no intellectual gifts, not even common sense, with which to face her appalling frustrations. For the first years of marriage her teenage husband, Louis XVI, was impotent. In Annunziata Asquith's words, 'Marie Antoinette had no other consolation than to abandon herself to amusement. Sadness and frivolity, gaiety and bad temper followed each other with unpredictable frequency, much to the alarm of Maria Theresa who did not guess the reason.'

But once the shades of the political prison-house begin literally to close upon her, we watch with total involvement the emergence of an indomitable spirit. Her dignity and courage evoked an instinct to serve her in such disparate characters as Baron de Tilly, Madame de Staël and Mirabeau, not to mention many of her jailers.

In a story where all the main actors are young, Annunziata Asquith has aimed at directness, simplicity and speed. Events race towards us. From the very start the narrative pace hints at the magnetic power of the dreadful climax ahead. We do not doubt that the drama she is unfolding with almost photographic vividness, did in fact happen as she relates. This is partly accomplished by a skilful use of quotations. Scarcely a paragraph passes without our hearing a voice from a diary, letter or memoir. At the same time, Annunziata Asquith misses none of the subtler theatrical effects, nor of the steps in the tragedy. There are the omens: the Lisbon earthquake, the blotted signature, the firework disaster and the blood-red or weeping skies. Then there is the progress of the Revolution itself, perhaps the world's most agonizing display of 'stop-go'. Above all there is the royal family's sleep-walking journey to the precipice, where accident and hatred took over for the last fatal push. Equally striking is Annunziata Asquith's handling of the great set pieces. Dumas and Carlyle, who in two classics have made the famous episodes of the Queen's Necklace and the Flight to Varennes peculiarly their own, would surely approve of the well-documented accounts in this book.

As in all revolutionary sagas whether English, French or Russian, we are left with an amazed incredulity. How could royal families have shown such folly; how could the victims of their supposed heartlessness have retaliated with such brutality? Marie Antoinette's brief life was a morality play, but with all the splendour of grand opera. Not only do the notorious *tricoteuses* of the French Revolution appear to advantage – or disadvantage – in these pages, but we are given the extra benefit of the '8,000 Judiths' of tigerish unfemininity marching on Versailles. The cold-blooded corrupting of little King Louis XVII by his revolutionary guards is strongly reminiscent of modern dictatorships.

'Too little and too late' can be seen as the moral. The Queen's children came too late to stabilize her and focus her 'giddiness' away from Vanity Fair. Her economies were too little; her attempts at escape too late. Too late also was the King's switch from a boorish obsession with machinery to an interest in books. In other matters, we see that the operative word with the King was 'nothing', rather than 'little' or 'late'. *Rien* – nothing – was a characteristic entry in his diary, whether for his wedding night or Bastille Day.

Yet when all is said, the death of Marie Antoinette does indeed purge us with pity and terror. In a sense the story, despite its horror, has a happy conclusion, since her end was so much more admirable than her beginning. As Annunziata Asquith writes: 'The discipline of extreme unhappiness and misfortune had at last made the Queen come to her senses.' No longer in our imagination do we see her as 'Madame Déficit' or 'Madame Veto' or 'the Baker's wife'. She is for all time the 'delightful vision' of Edmund Burke, 'glittering like the morning star'. Burke had once thought that ten thousand swords would have leaped from their scabbards in her just cause. Annunziata Asquith, without ever losing sight of reality, has achieved the same result with her pen.

Elizabeth Longford

1 Crossing of the Rhine

1755-70

IN THE LAST DAYS of October 1755 Austrian messengers reached Lisbon with a formal request from Maria Theresa, Queen of Bohemia and Hungary, Empress of the Holy Roman Empire, to the King and Queen of Portugal that they should be god-parents to her fifteenth child, the child she was shortly expecting. Only eight of her children, so far, had grown to maturity. Five were daughters; she was hoping this time for a son.

Confined to her chamber in the Hofburg Palace of Vienna, she used the time to practical advantage. To the last moment she followed the normal pattern of her daily life, hardly resting as she checked her files, dictated letters and read the documents brought for her signature. When she was finally forced to put down her pen, she summoned a dentist to remove a tooth which had been troubling her for some time.

Late in the afternoon of 2 November, All Souls' Day, the Emperor Francis of Lorraine was still attending High Mass when he was hurriedly summoned to his wife's bedside. Towards half-past seven in the evening a little girl was born, their sixth daughter and ninth surviving child: Maria Antonia Josephina Johanna. The *Te Deum* was sung, the child was blessed and then presented to the assembled Court in the Hall of Mirrors. Soon afterwards she was removed to a distant wing of the Hofburg Palace where Marie Constance Hoffmann, her nurse, and a few ladies of the nobility were to take care of her.

None of the Court assembled at her christening ceremony the following day knew that her god-parents that very moment were fleeing in terror from their palace in Lisbon. A violent earthquake had just destroyed the town and buried thirty thousand beneath the smoking ruins. But a strange hesitation, none the less, hung over the Court. Francis of Lorraine was obsessed by premonitions and could not bring himself to give the great public banquet normal at the birth of an archduchess. Instead, he had the baby's horoscope drawn by Gassner, then famous in Vienna for his inspired prophecies. This time, however, he could only be prevailed upon to remark that 'there are crosses for all shoulders' before he turned pale and would say no more. The dreadful news from Lisbon cast an extra shadow and, years later, when the turn of events had long proved the case, these early signs of foreboding were taken as unmistakable pointers to the dark future.

Maria Theresa had already taken up her files and resumed the affairs of state. When van Swieten, her doctor, suggested that she might enjoy a few quiet days with her family after this latest

LEFT Leopold Mozart with
Wolfgang and Nannerl: a
watercolour by Louis
Carrogis de Carmontelle of
their appearance in public
in 1763, when Wolfgang was
only seven.

The Habsburg children
receiving St Nicholas's Day
gifts in 1762: the painting is
reputedly by the
Archduchess Maria Christina
after C. Troots, and shows
the Emperor and Empress
by the table.

childbirth, she had refused. 'My subjects are my first children,' she replied. 'My first care must be for them; the others must come after.'

Maria Theresa was now in her thirty-seventh year. Fourteen years earlier she had come to the throne to find a coalition of European powers firmly bent on dividing her states among themselves. One by one the signatories to those treaties by which her father, Charles VI, had tried to secure her succession to the Holy Roman Empire, had abandoned her. The Prussians had defeated the Austrian forces at Mollwitz, France and Bavaria prepared to carve up the Habsburg Empire. In Paris, Cardinal Fleury announced to the world: 'There is no more House of Austria.' But they counted without the remarkable courage and determination of the new Queen, a young girl barely twenty-three years old. 'Gentlemen, why such gloomy faces?' she asked the old men round her council table as she set out on an almost impossible task to bring order and unification to her fragmented and multilingual realm.

For her youngest daughter, Marie Antoinette – as she was known after the signing of the marriage contract with the Dauphin on 4 April 1770 – a role of political opportunity was to exist almost from the moment of birth. For a century and a half Bourbons and Habsburgs had fought each other for European predominance. But France now seemed far less of a menace than Frederick of Prussia, the ambitious Protestant power in northern Germany. 'Le Monstre', as Maria Theresa bitterly named her unwelcome neighbour, had lost no time in seizing Silesia, Austria's richest province, on the death of the Emperor Charles VI in 1740. In the short interval between the close of the War of Austrian Succession in 1748 and the outbreak of the Seven Years War in 1756, both Austria and France came to realize that their long tradition of hostility was now outdated.

It was a proof of the position which Frederick, in so few years, had gained for Prussia that his own change of front altered the political face of Europe. In May 1756, four months after Prussia and England had signed the Treaty of Westminster, the Houses of Habsburg and Bourbon, for the first time in centuries, found themselves united for joint action. Hardly had the news of the Prussian alliance reached Paris when Austria was asked whether she was ready to abandon her alliance with England if France, in her turn, would renounce that of Prussia. By the Treaty of Versailles in May 1756 Maria Theresa at last succeeded in establishing relations of friendship between herself and the French Court.

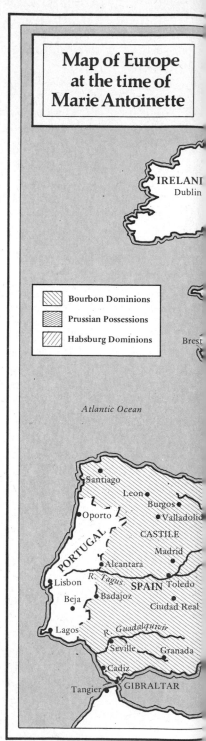

Map of Europe at the time of Marie Antoinette

Bourbon Dominions
Prussian Possessions
Habsburg Dominions

IRELAND
Dublin

Brest

Atlantic Ocean

Santiago
Leon
Burgos
Oporto
Valladolid
PORTUGAL
CASTILE
Madrid
Alcantara
R. Tagus
Lisbon
SPAIN
Toledo
Beja
Badajoz
Ciudad Real
Lagos
R. Guadalquivir
Seville
Granada
Cadiz
Tangier
GIBRALTAR

'Never', she said, 'during my whole reign have I signed a treaty with so cheerful a heart.'

It had been the work of two men in particular: the Prince of Kaunitz, Austrian ambassador to Versailles in 1753 and later Chancellor of the Empire, and the Duke of Choiseul, French ambassador to Vienna and later Louis XV's chief minister. To them, it became evident that this alliance, born of necessity, needed a far stronger guarantee than a shred of paper to ensure good relations between the traditional enemies. The most natural solution was to betroth the young Dauphin, grandson of Louis XV, to a daughter of Maria Theresa. Marie Antoinette, ten years old, was the most suitable in age. On 24 May 1766 Stahremberg, the Austrian ambassador in Paris, wrote to the Empress: 'The King has spoken in such a way that your Majesty can regard the matter as settled.'

In the anonymity of the palace nurseries, a slender, fair-haired child was too busy playing truant from her lessons to be aware of

ABOVE The exquisite palace of Schönbrunn, home of the Habsburgs: a painting by Bernardo Bellotto, the nephew of Canaletto.

RIGHT An early portrait of Marie Antoinette, aged about nine.

her important diplomatic role. Cold winter days in the cheerless Hofburg Palace gave way soon enough to the freedom that later seasons offered at Schönbrunn, only a few miles from Vienna. There, Marie Antoinette and her sister Caroline led a wild, almost carefree existence, riding on sledges through the woods or playing tirelessly with their pet dogs. They grew skilful in evading the threats of Countess von Brandeiss, the governess, who tried in vain to bring a little discipline to their lives. Marie Antoinette even persuaded her to write out her schoolroom exercises in pencil so that she could trace them over in ink later. Countess Lerchenfeld, appointed as her successor when Maria Theresa found out, was scarcely less indulgent. Contemporary prints made much of the superior talents of Maria Theresa's children, noting how the younger princesses appeared to answer fluently in Latin when addressed in that language. If they did, they certainly understood not a word. The sum of Marie Antoinette's knowledge was pitiful: a little Italian from Metastasio, the poet and librettist, a little music from Gluck and a smattering of French. A tomboy and a mimic, she was restless and naturally lazy, too easily distracted to be more than a stranger to learning.

It was a childhood she remembered with real happiness, clouded only for the first time by her father's death on 18 August 1765. At Innsbruck, while attending the marriage of his son Leopold, Grand Duke of Tuscany, he had an apoplectic fit and died in his eldest son Joseph's arms. Marie Antoinette never forgot his last farewell to her. Already his carriage had left the Palace and was on the road to Innsbruck when he sent a messenger back for his youngest daughter. Taking the child of nine in his arms, he held her tightly. 'God knows, gentlemen,' he said, 'how I wanted to embrace this child once more.' It was the last he saw of her but he had taken the precaution of leaving behind a list of instructions to be read by his children twice a year, warning them, among other things, against false friendships. It was soon to be laid aside and forgotten.

To Francis of Lorraine, his children had been a source of real pleasure and companionship. Their mother, on the other hand, was a more remote figure, one who inspired fear and respect rather than love. From five in the summer mornings and six in the winter, she devoted herself to the administration of high politics. Impervious to the cold, she sat at her desk, often letting the fire go out altogether as she worked. Windows and doors were flung open even in mid-winter, making the cold so intense that Joseph, her eldest son, would come to her apartments well wrapped in furs. She would try to see her children at the end of the morning but often she relied on van Swieten, her doctor, who went daily to visit the young imperial family and reported back on their health.

When a stranger of rank arrived in Vienna, the Empress would cluster her family round her table, giving the false impression that she personally supervised her children's education. Instead, she sent written instructions to the governesses. So far as her six daughters were concerned, it seems never to have crossed her mind to provide them with adequate teaching. She, who complained in later years of her own narrow and useless education, inflicted much the same sort of upbringing on her own daughters. Marie Antoinette, in particular, was never taught to use her mind at all. Her lessons were dull and learned in parrot-fashion, following much the same sort of timetable as given to her elder sisters:

Getting up at 7.30. From 8.30 on, penmanship, reading, spelling. Holy Mass at 10.0. French lesson at 11.0. Dinner at noon. Three times a week, from 2–3, Fr. Richter. On the other weekdays, this hour for maps, some history, some books and fables. Needlework and the like till 4.0. At 5.0 Rosary in Church (every day). Evenings: games, callers, sometimes Theatre.

From a distance their upbringing was rigidly prescribed. The first quality the Empress required of her daughters was obedience:

They are born to obey and must learn to do so in good time. Never must they be allowed to be afraid, neither of thunderstorms, fire, ghosts, witches, or any other nonsense . . . you are not to let them be frightened of illness so you will talk in a perfectly natural way of everything of this kind, even smallpox and death. . . . They must not be allowed to show aversion to anything, still less to anybody: no familiarity with the servants, politeness to all and particularly towards strangers.

She demanded obedience sometimes to the point of excess. Marie Antoinette, eleven at the time, remembered with horror how her sister Maria Josephina, engaged to the King of Naples, had been forbidden by Maria Theresa to leave Vienna before praying at the family tomb. The child regarded this order as a certain death-warrant as her brother Joseph's second wife, Josephine of Bavaria, had recently been interred there after dying from a smallpox attack. In tears, the bride had taken Marie Antoinette on her lap and said her last goodbye before she went down to the crypt. Her fears were realized when, two weeks later, she died of smallpox

The imperial capital, Vienna:
ABOVE The splendour of the
Spanish Hofreitschule
(riding school) in Vienna,
1743: this painting, of the
school of Meytens, shows a
'carroussel' for horsewomen
in progress.

LEFT A contemporary view of
the famous Prater in Vienna.
From Carl Schuetz's
*Sammlung von Aussichten der
Residenzstadt Wien.*

An imperial performance of Gluck's *Il Parnasso confuso* at Schönbrunn in January 1765: Archduke (later Emperor) Joseph is at the spinet, and the painting is by J. F. Greipel.

on the very day she was to have left Vienna on her journey across the Alps. If Marie Antoinette was heartbroken at the loss, her mother was more practical. Undaunted, she sent another daughter, Maria Carolina, to fill the dead girl's place.

Despite the severity of the rules, there was still a great deal of time for amusements. So much so that Khevenhuller, Chamberlain of the Viennese Court, gloomily asked himself in his diary whether so much play-acting, dancing, singing and dressing-up might not turn their Highnesses into flibberty-gibbets. Sometimes the children would be entertained by performances other than their own. In 1762 the child Mozart and his sister Marianne were commanded by Maria Theresa to appear at Schönbrunn. Delighted, Leopold Mozart wrote to his wife in Salzburg to describe the meeting: 'Now, there is only time to tell you that we were so graciously received that as I tell it it will be reckoned a fairy-tale. Let it suffice that Wolferl sprang on the lap of the Empress, put his arms around her neck and vigorously kissed her. We were with her

22

from three o'clock to six.' Leopold allowed himself to expect great things from the Empress. But Maria Theresa was happy to be amused by the child; of the genius she was unaware.

Other things preyed on her mind. Three years after Stahremberg's declaration that the marriage question was 'settled', no further arrangements had been concluded. The Austrian Court was apparently more eager to clinch the deal. The Marquis de Durfort, French ambassador to Vienna, was made the central object of attention. The Empress showered little gifts on him such as pears and peaches in January, and would subject him to edifying, and no doubt fabricated, recommendations of her daughter's progress: 'Over which European country would you prefer to be Queen?' asks the Empress. 'France,' replies Marie Antoinette without a moment's hesitation, 'because it is the country of Henry IV and Louis XIV, the one so good, the other so great.' At Marie Antoinette's birthday fête, a blazing dolphin (Dauphin) ended the display of fireworks. It was a strong enough hint, but still Louis XV hesitated to commit himself.

Early in 1769, Joseph Ducreux, a little-known pastellist chosen by Choiseul for economy's sake, arrived in Vienna. He had instructions from the King of France to paint the portraits of three Archduchesses and even of a son-in-law of the Empress, thereby masking the real purpose of the mission. Two months later, Durfort's son rode post-haste to Versailles with Marie Antoinette's portrait. The pastel had its desired effect: in June 1769 Louis XV formally asked for Marie Antoinette's hand in marriage to the Dauphin, his grandson, and suggested Easter 1770 for the celebration of the wedding.

It was about this time that Maria Theresa discovered to her horror that the future Queen of France, now thirteen years old, had by-passed learning altogether. There was less than a year left in which to remedy the situation. It was essential that she should become a good dancer and be able to speak French with a perfect accent. Noverre, the famous dancing-master of the Paris opera, was hastily engaged, and two French actors, Aufresne and Sainville, then playing in Vienna, were to teach her elocution and French singing. When Versailles learned to their horror that the future Dauphine was being instructed by 'strolling players', Abbé Vermond, Doctor in the Sorbonne, was sent out to Vienna as tutor.

He set to work with courage and tact. His pupil hated reading, wrote very badly, spelled worse and spoke French with an atrocious accent. It was uphill work: 'A little laziness and much frivolity make it very difficult for me to teach the Archduchess.

She understands perfectly well when I put clear ideas before her. Her judgement is always good but I cannot get her into the way of exploring a question although I know she is capable of it.' He found he could get results only by 'amusing' his pupil, for, though she was eager to learn, her mocking nature and constant love of distraction 'counteracted her talent for learning'. Writing she was never to find amusing: 'I must confess this is the subject in which I have made least progress,' but with French history he was more fortunate. She began to learn the lives of the Queens of France, the genealogy of the Bourbons and the principal offices of the Court of Versailles. She even took an interest in the French army. 'I am convinced', wrote Vermond enthusiastically 'that in a very little time after her marriage her Royal Highness will know every colonel by name and be able to distinguish each regiment by its uniform and colours.'

Usually hard of praise, he soon grew very fond of his little pupil and wrote happily to the Comte de Mercy-Argenteau, Austrian Ambassador in Paris, that 'The Court and the Nation will be charmed with our future Dauphine.' 'You might find faces which are more regularly beautiful', he remarked, 'but I doubt if you would find one more attractive.' There were, however, certain imperfections of her appearance that had to be improved. For three months she had to suffer Laveran, the French dentist recommended by Vermond, while he corrected the set of her teeth. Her hair was an added problem. It grew too low down on her forehead and caused great anxiety to the Empress. Larseneur, a French hairdresser sent over by Choiseul, managed to invent a new hairstyle which she was to wear in her portrait by Ducreux. The Count of Neny, Maria Theresa's private secretary, described it as 'simple and decent but at the same time very flattering to the face'. He was sure that young ladies would soon 'abandon their mountains of curls and dress their hair like the Dauphine'. As her marriage drew nearer, she was relentlessly drilled in the regulation curtsies of Versailles and interminable Court etiquette. Even Kaunitz grew impressed with her progress, immersed as he was in his struggles with Choiseul and Durfort to settle the problems of ceremonial to the satisfaction of both the Austrian and French sides.

Two months before her wedding, the fourteen-year-old child still had no image of her future husband other than the blazing Dolphin of a firelit sky. The Empress asked Durfort to send a portrait of her son-in-law. From Versailles came three engravings

of *The Dauphin ploughing*, hardly suitable for such an occasion. A month later, following Maria Theresa's remonstrations, two portraits of Louis Auguste in ceremonial dress were given to Marie Antoinette who asked permission to hang hers up 'in the room where she sits'. 'I cannot tell you how much satisfaction these portraits have given,' wrote Durfort with obvious relief. Maria Theresa was less enthusiastic than her daughter. After studying the portraits, she remarked aphoristically to the girl that: 'Domestic happiness consists of mutual trust and kindness. Passionate love soon disappears.' Mercy was less tactful: 'Nature', he said, 'seems to have denied everything to Monsieur le Dauphin' and he seemed moreover to possess 'only a limited amount of sense'.

For the past year Marie Antoinette's training had been rigorous but not entirely successful. Maria Theresa was under no illusions concerning her youngest daughter: 'I realized that her character comprised much frivolity, lack of application and obstinacy in following her own will, together with adroitness in evading

The Dauphin Ploughing: one of the uninspiring engravings sent to the Empress Maria Theresa as a likeness of Louis Auguste.

25

intended reproaches.' A few days before she was to leave Vienna, Maria Theresa moved the girl into her own bedroom, hoping to the last to make a Queen out of this stubborn and headstrong child.

On Easter Sunday, 15 April 1770, the Marquis de Durfort made his public entrance as Envoy Extraordinary of Louis XV. Forty-eight coaches rolled through the streets of Vienna as Marie Antoinette and her sister Maria Christina watched from an upstairs window. They scanned the cortège for the two royal travelling-coaches, a gift from Louis XV to his future grand-daughter-in-law. They had been made by the saddler Francien after Choiseul's own design and were upholstered in crimson and blue velvet. They were embroidered inside with the four seasons, while on top bouquets of flowers in gold of different colours waved gracefully in the slightest breeze. The cost of the procession had been enormous. Durfort had spent 350,000 ducats, of which half had come from his own pocket. The presentation coaches were empty, but in the others were his officers surrounded by pages, grooms and servants, 117 persons in all, dressed in 'rich stuffs', Durfort's livery of blue, yellow and silver. Immediately afterwards, he sold the entire stable to help recoup some of his expenses.

On the following day he presented a new request for Marie Antoinette's hand in marriage, and watched her perform her first political act: the renunciation of the hereditary Austrian succession. On Thursday, 19 April, at six in the evening, the trumpets sounded as the entire Court made its way through the gallery of the Hofburg to the Church of the Augustines where the marriage by proxy was to take place. Archduke Ferdinand, seventeen months older than his sister, took the bridegroom's place as the girl, in her dress of cloth-of-silver, knelt beside her mother and became Dauphine of France. There was a burst of cannon and musketry as the *Te Deum* was sung. Already the Comte de Lorge, Durfort's son, was galloping towards Versailles with the news.

Two days later, at half-past nine in the morning, the carriages were drawn up outside the Hofburg Palace. For the last time the Empress took her daughter in her arms. Marie Antoinette, overcome with sorrow, was carried half-fainting to the door of her carriage by the Archduke Ferdinand. As she disappeared from sight, Maria Theresa knelt in church to pray for her daughter's future. Already her letter was on its way to Louis XV: 'She has the best will in the world, but she is so young. Pray forgive her if she is sometimes a trifle giddy and careless.'

From early in the morning the crowds had lined the streets of

26

Vienna to watch the departure. They watched as she passed by, 'her cheeks bathed in tears, lying back in her coach, covering her eyes, sometimes with her handkerchief and sometimes with her hands; now and then putting her head out of the carriage to take another look at the palace of her ancestors which she was never more to enter'.

The huge cavalcade of 376 horses, fifty-seven carriages and a retinue of 132 set slowly out on the road through upper Austria and across Bavaria on the way to Strasbourg and the imperial frontier. It was cold and raining when fifteen days later they reached the Abbey of Schüttern, near Kehl, where Marie Antoinette was to spend her last night on Austrian soil. The handing-over ceremony was to take place on neutral ground, in a temporary wooden lodge built on the Ile des Epis at Strasbourg's gates between the two arms of the Rhine. Huge tapestries borrowed from the old Cardinal de Rohan, Archbishop of Strasbourg, hid the rough wooden planking. Goethe, then aged twenty, a student of law in Strasbourg, who had come to visit the room before the ceremony, had been horrified by their choice of subject: they showed the story of Jason and Medea, 'the most horrible marriage that can be imagined'.

Just before midday on 7 May, the Dauphine crossed the Rhine bridge at Kehl and arrived at the makeshift lodge. She changed her travelling clothes for a ceremonial dress before she entered the *salle de remise* and stood before the crimson-covered table which symbolized the frontier. On the other side were only three people: the Comte de Noailles, governor of Versailles, and two assistants. Behind her the door giving on to Germany remained open. The French door was still shut. The ceremony lasted only a few minutes before the Austrian ladies kissed her hand and left by the German door which was then closed behind them. The French door opened and Marie Antoinette, surrounded by strangers, threw herself into the arms of her new lady-in-waiting, the Comtesse de Noailles. She left the lodge in her coach with the golden flowers and entered Strasbourg, the first town to welcome her to France.

From the first moment, Marie Antoinette charmed the French with her grace and good breeding. Addressed in German, she was quick to interrupt: 'Do not speak German, gentlemen. From today I understand no language but French.' In the absence of the old Cardinal de Rohan, a strange prelate received the girl on the porch of the cathedral. Prince Louis de Rohan, Bishop coadjutor of the diocese, was later to become the key figure in the most serious

27

scandal of her reign. It was he who now gave the child her first blessing on French soil.

The Baroness of Oberkirche, from Alsace, saw her for the first time that day. Years later she was to write:

At that time, Her Highness the Dauphine was tall and well-made, although a little slim. She has changed but little since then; her face is still the same, long, with regular features and aquiline nose although it has a Roman bridge; a high forehead and lovely blue eyes. Her tiny mouth already seemed slightly disdainful . . . she had the Austrian lip. . . . Nothing can describe her dazzling complexion, literally milk and roses. Everything about her betokened the greatness of her line and her gentleness and nobility of heart. She appealed to all.

For a week the Dauphine journeyed across eastern France, through Commercy, Châlons, Reims and Soissons, stoically enduring a never-ending series of triumphal arches, firework displays, theatrical productions and military parades. The *Gazette de France* marvelled at her gentle gaiety and dignified affability, while Mercy wrote to the Empress: 'Our Archduchess-Dauphiness has surpassed all my hopes.'

From dawn on 14 May 1770, large crowds had been gathering on the outskirts of the forest of Compiègne. By the Pont de Berne where, thirty-six years later, Napoleon was to wait for Marie-Louise, Louis XV and his Court waited to greet Marie Antoinette. As the evening drew on, the sound of trumpets and drums signalled her approach. The gold-flowered carriage had hardly stopped when the Dauphine jumped out. Hurrying ahead of Choiseul who had gone to meet her, she threw herself at the King's feet – he raised her up and embraced her. The Dauphine then turned with interest to the boy who was already her husband. According to etiquette he kissed her on the cheek though the situation seemed clearly to increase his awkwardness and lack of confidence.

Shy and clumsy, he was not yet sixteen and seemed really happy only when engaged in some strenuous feat of manual labour such as sawing wood or making locks. Hunting was the only other thing for which he showed any real enthusiasm. Women alarmed him. '*Ce n'est pas un homme comme un autre*' ('He is not like other men'), remarked his grandfather with sarcasm. He was not stupid by any means; he studied history and geography with interest and knew some Latin, Italian, German and English, but he had been kept so much in the background that his appearances at Court were an ordeal. He suffered from an inferiority complex and a resulting paralysis of will which he was never to overcome. His character was beyond reproach but his graces were lacking. In the scanty diary which he had kept since his thirteenth year, the only entry for that evening ran: '*Entrevue avec Madame la Dauphine*'.

Also at Compiègne to meet the new Dauphine were a selection of the most unpleasant set of relations she could have hoped to acquire. Mesdames Adelaide, Victoire and Sophie, her new aunts, the unmarried daughters of Louis xv, were to use Marie Antoinette as a puppet in their absurd intrigues and spiteful quarrels at Versailles. Adelaide, the eldest, had ranked as 'first lady' and naturally resented being dethroned by this Austrian girl. Others present were the Duc d'Orleans, the Duc de Bourbon and his son the Duc de Chartres, who years later sided with the revolutionaries, voting for Louis xvi's death, only to suffer the same fate soon after.

A portrait of Marie Antoinette in oils by J. Baptiste Charpentier, after the appealing pastel by Joseph Ducreux.

From Compiègne, the procession went on to the Château de La Muette, a royal hunting-lodge in the Bois de Boulogne. It was to be the last stopping-place before Versailles. Here Marie Antoinette was to meet the Comte de Provence and Comte d'Artois, the Dauphin's younger brothers. Their sisters Clothilde and Elisabeth waited at Versailles. That evening, at the formal banquet given in her honour, she was to meet Madame du Barry, the King's mistress, illegitimate daughter of a seamstress and now the most influential woman in Versailles. For the first time she had been included in a state function. 'It seems inconceivable', Mercy wrote to Maria Theresa, 'that the King should choose this moment to grant his favourite an honour which has hitherto been refused her.' Of her position Marie Antoinette was unaware and innocently leaned over to ask the Comtesse de Noailles. The lady-of-honour hesitated and then said: 'Her office . . . to amuse the King.' 'Then I shall be her rival,' rejoined Marie Antoinette instantly. Perhaps it was to forestall the bad impression that Louis xv presented his grand-daughter that evening with a magnificent set of diamonds.

At nine o'clock the following morning Marie Antoinette left for Versailles where the final marriage ceremony was to take place. All day long five thousand people had gathered in the Hall of Mirrors and the chapel to witness the spectacle. On 16 May only those whose birth gave them a right to attend, were present. Normally, Versailles was an open theatre. Only 'dogs, mendicant friars and people newly marked with smallpox' could not cross the threshold of the Salon of Hercules. Sightseers with no hat and sword were also turned back, a situation easily remedied by the

29

concierge who did a roaring trade in these accessories. 'Loose women' were admitted on condition they did not ply their 'shameful trade' in the apartments. Only in their private apartments were the royal family secure from intrusion and constant surveillance.

At one o'clock the ceremony began. Dressed in rose, gold and silver, the Dauphine walked through the Hall of Mirrors and Grand Apartments, hand in hand with Louis Auguste who seemed nervous and ill-at-ease in his gold braid and diamonds. At the end of the Nuptial Mass the parish priest of Versailles brought in the marriage register. Slowly and painfully Marie Antoinette added her name to the signatures of Louis XV and the Dauphin. Her hand trembled as she tried to form the letters in her childish hand, and a large ink blot dropped from her pen to obscure the last few letters. The Dauphin's brothers, Mesdames and the Orleans family followed. Each as they signed could see at the head of the page the untidy scrawl which the child, whose arrival they all feared, left as a record of her fifteenth year.

That evening, in the new opera-house that Louis XV had commissioned from Gabriel in Marie Antoinette's honour, twenty-two people sat down for dinner watched by a crowd of six thousand. Marie Antoinette hardly touched her food while the Dauphin steadily devoured every dish that was set before him. The King leaned anxiously towards him: 'Don't overload your stomach tonight.' 'Why not?' asked his grandson, 'I always sleep better after a good supper.' Louis XV looked with pity at Marie Antoinette.

The following day the Dauphin wrote one word in his diary: '*Rien*', an entry that was to continue with disturbing persistency. Two days after his wedding he left the bed at dawn to go hunting. He came back exhausted, to find Marie Antoinette playing with a little dog. 'Have you slept well?' he asked her. 'Yes,' she answered. There was no further conversation between them. Vermond, who was in the room, wrote: 'The Dauphine played with her little dog. He served as a diversion for a moment, then she fell to musing. My heart was wrung.' On the third night of marriage again 'nothing' happened. Mercy, who prided himself on his medical knowledge, tried to explain to Maria Theresa that 'the Dauphin's development is late probably because his construction has been weakened by his sudden and rapid growth'.

The festivities continued none the less. Ten days after the wedding they were to reach their peak as the crowds gathered at nightfall to watch the firework display. The bride and groom, the King and Mercy, stood at the central window of the Hall of Mirrors

Louis XV aged thirty-eight: a pastel by Maurice Quentin de la Tour. Superficially elegant and sensual by nature, Louis could not help but despise the inadequacies of his grandson.

to watch the rockets which in their thousands painted in the sky the arms of the Dauphin and Dauphine. 'The great bouquet at the end', noted Papillon de la Ferté, steward of the Light Amusements, 'consisted of twenty thousand rockets; it was the largest which had ever been seen.' A sun-temple had been erected at the end of the grand canal while musicians sat in torch-lit boats on the water below. Orchestras scattered through the park echoed their music as the crowds danced till six the next morning. Marie Antoinette, who made the rounds in a coach, was greeted everywhere with cries of joy. 'What do you think of my festivities?' the King asked Terray, his comptroller of finances. 'Sire, I think they are priceless.' The word he had used was '*impayables*'. Twenty years later, tradesmen at the beginning of the Revolution were still asking to be paid a fraction of what they had spent on these festivities.

As Dauphine, however, Marie Antoinette had emerged triumphant. 'She had such a graceful word for everyone and curtsied so prettily that in a few days she delighted everyone. . . . There is

One of the many firework displays that greeted Marie Antoinette along the route to Paris: a contemporary engraving.

31

OPPOSITE The archdukes and
archduchesses playing at
opera in the gardens of
Schönbrunn. The painting
is by an artist of the school
of Meytens.

a charm in her manner which will turn all our heads.' Even the stern Mercy admitted: 'She is all smiles.'

The culmination of the wedding festivities was to take place in Paris on the Place Louis XV, now the Place de la Concorde, on the night of 30 May. At eight o'clock in the evening Marie Antoinette, accompanied only by Madame Adelaide, set out from Versailles to watch the celebrations. The carriage had hardly crossed the Pont de Sèvres when the sky was filled with the light of exploding fireworks. A few moments later a terrible sound came from the direction of the square. People were running in terror from the Rue Royale where four hundred thousand were jammed in the surrounding streets. Carriages were overturned and horses suffocated as men, women and children stumbled and were trodden underfoot.

By the time Marie Antoinette was returning in tears to Versailles the panic had died down. The wounded were cared for and the dead taken away. In the morning the Dauphin, overcome with sorrow, sent his private expenses of the month to the Hôtel de Ville: 'It is all I have to give. I send it to you,' he wrote. 'Give aid to the most unfortunate.' Marie Antoinette followed his example.

That same morning, 132 labelled corpses were laid out in the cemetery of the Madeleine, on the same grass enclosure where, twenty-three years later, the body of Marie Antoinette would be thrown on the bare ground.

THE FESTIVITIES WERE OVER. Versailles relapsed into calm before the annual exodus of the Court to Marly, Choisy, Fontainebleau and Compiègne. Marie Antoinette became enmeshed in the routine of Court etiquette. To her mother she wrote a description of how she was expected to spend her day:

I get up at half-past nine or ten o'clock, dress and say my morning prayers. Then I have breakfast, and go to see my aunts, where I generally find the King. This takes until 10.30. Then at 11.0 I go to have my hair dressed. Next comes the *levée* which all may attend, except persons without rank or name. I rouge my cheeks and wash my hands before the assembled company; then the gentlemen withdraw, the ladies remain and I dress myself in their presence. Now, it is time for church. If the King is at Versailles I go with him, with my husband, and my aunts to Mass. If the King is away I go alone with the Dauphin, but always at the same time. After Mass we have our dinner in public but this is over by 1.30 for we both eat very quickly. Then I am with the Dauphin for a time, and when he has business to do I retire to my own room, where I read, write or work. Needlework, for I am embroidering the King a coat which gets forward very slowly though I hope with God's grace it will be finished in a few years from now. At 3.0 I go again to my aunts' where the King is at this hour. At 4.0 the Abbé comes to me and at 5.0 my Clavecin teacher or singing-master till 6.0. At 6.30 I almost always go to my aunts unless I go out. I should tell you that my husband almost always goes with me to my aunts'. From 7.0 till 9.0 we play cards; but when it is fine I go out, and then the cards are not in my room but at my aunts'. At 9.0 we have supper and when the King is not there the aunts have supper with us. When the King is there we go to the aunts after supper. We wait there for the King who usually comes at about a quarter to eleven. While waiting I lie down on a big sofa and go to sleep until the King comes. When he is away we go to bed at 11.0. This is how I spend my day.

Unknown to Marie Antoinette, the Empress, far off in Schönbrunn, was keeping the minutest watch on this foreign Court. To protect her daughter from the snares of palace intrigue she had sent the ablest of her diplomats, Count Mercy, as her ambassador and counsellor in Paris. With singular frankness she wrote to him: 'I dread my daughter's youth, the effect which undue flattery may have upon her, her idleness and her lack of any inclination for serious activity. Let me urge you to keep a watchful eye upon these matters and to see to it that she does not fall into bad hands – for I have every confidence in you.'

Special messengers brought his detailed reports to Vienna. Marked *'tibi soli'* ('for you alone'), the letters were kept even from

PREVIOUS PAGES The magnificent château of St Cloud, seen from the Grande Avenue: the engraving is by J. Rigaud.

OPPOSITE Marie Antoinette, by Le Maître des portraits des archiduchesses.

37

Marie Antoinette's first letter to her mother after her arrival in Paris, dated 12 July 1770.

OPPOSITE Marie Antoinette's brother Joseph at the harpsichord, with two of the archduchesses. This painting, by an Austrian Court painter, dates from about 1785.

Kaunitz and the Emperor Joseph, and through them the Empress followed her daughter's every movement. Mercy had cast a fine-meshed net around his protégée:

I have made sure of three persons in the service of the Archduchess: one of her women and two of her menservants, who give me full reports of what goes on. Then, from day to day, I am told of the conversations she has with Abbé Vermond, from whom she hides nothing. Besides this, the Marquise de Durfort passes on to me everything she says to her aunts. I also have sources of information as to what goes on whenever the Dauphine sees the King. Added to this are my personal observations so that there really is not an hour of the day as to which I am not instructed concerning what the Archduchess may have said, or done, or heard. . . . I have made my enquiries this extensive because I know how essential it is to your Majesty's tranquillity that you should be fully informed.

It was curious that Marie Antoinette never suspected the source of the secret information of which she was the victim. The Empress, after each rebuke, was careful to say that Mercy was in no way responsible for details concerning Marie Antoinette's behaviour, but that they were obtained through some mysterious secret agency. The Dauphine believed her mother implicitly and thus lived in perpetual mistrust of all around her. 'Madame la Dauphine', wrote Vermond, 'does not feel that any paper belonging to her is safe. She is afraid of skeleton keys and fancies that her own keys are taken from her pockets at night. She is quite obsessed with

The Comte de Mercy-
Argenteau: a contemporary
portrait. To this devoted
Austrian ambassador, Maria
Theresa owed her knowledge
of the minutest details of
her daughter's life in Paris.

these perhaps imaginary terrors.' Unconnected incidents such as the following only served to intensify her fears. The Duc de la Vauguyon had been the Dauphin's tutor and now resented his declining influence over his former pupil: 'Something very odd has just happened,' Marie Antoinette told her mother, 'I was alone with my husband when M. de la Vauguyon hurried up to the door to listen. One of the *valets de chambre*, who is either a fool or a very honest man, opened the door and Monsieur le Duc was left standing there like a post without being able to escape. So I mentioned to my husband the disadvantage there was in letting people listen at doors and he took it very well.'

From every direction the Dauphine was the object of tireless scrutiny. Maria Theresa, for her part, was trying too late to atone for her previous lack of interest by safeguarding her daughter from the whims of her unruly nature. Madame de Noailles, attached to the Dauphine's household as lady-in-waiting, had a thankless task. Prim and snobbish even by the standards of the *Ancien Régime*, she had, according to Mercy, 'so little character or cleverness that it is impossible to make her see reason as regards the best means of discharging her duties'. She was soon nicknamed 'Madame l'Etiquette' by Marie Antoinette who then made her life miserable by taunting her with impossible questions of protocol, demanding to know the correct procedure should a Dauphine fall off her donkey.

In the daily routine of Versailles there was little place left for amusements and it was these she missed most of all. Her mother's resoluteness was only partly successful in curbing her rebellious spirit. 'The worst thing she does', wrote Mercy to the Empress, 'is listen to the advice given by Mesdames. She is careless of her appearance and bored by ceremonial which she avoids whenever she can.' He was soon warning Maria Theresa: 'Madame la Dauphine is careless of outward appearances . . . she makes fun of people who appear to her ridiculous.' The Ambassador often noticed her 'whispering in the ears of the young ladies' and then 'laughing with them'. Maria Theresa remonstrated with her: 'By amusing five or six young ladies or gentlemen you will lose the rest.' Louis XV, when informed of his grand-daughter's mockery, did not hide his displeasure: 'It is quite right that in private Madame la Dauphine should give way to her natural gaiety, but in public when she is holding her court, her behaviour must be more reserved.'

But the Dauphine's lively nature refused to be curbed. She

decided she would like to ride. Mercy, whom this idea frightened 'in view of the Dauphine's extreme youth', warned Choiseul, who went to tell Louis XV. The King, bored by the whole affair, compromised, and allowed her to ride a donkey, which after several happy expeditions to Compiègne became a pony and then a horse. Mercy proposed a middle course: 'That the Archduchess should go only at a walking pace and rarely trot.' Maria Theresa tried every tactic: 'Riding spoils the complexion,' she wrote. But it was in vain. 'The donkeys and horses will have occupied the time needed for reading,' but at least let her daughter not go hunting. The girl promised, but at the beginning of May 1771 she disobeyed on the pretext of having 'accidently met the hunt'. She then repeated the offence, following the hunt on horseback or in a cabriolet, which frightened Maria Theresa still more. The fifteen-year-old child began to play the part of caterer. 'Her Royal Highness', Mercy reported, 'has the habit of bringing in her carriages all kinds of cold meats and refreshments which she likes to distribute to the courtiers following the hunt.'

It was a constant battle of will. Even the fact that Marie Antoinette had stopped wearing a whalebone corset led to an exchange of numerous letters between Versailles and Vienna. After a long series of maternal admonitions, Mercy could at last report: 'Madame la Dauphine is again wearing her whalebone corset.' 'Her carelessness, her lack of pleasure in any serious concentration and her indiscretion provide me with many occasions of anxiety,' wrote Maria Theresa with alarm.

One evil came from her intimacy with her aunts. Neglected by her husband, whose marital failures had plunged him further into awkwardness and misanthropy, the little girl had no other resources than to go four or five times a day to see Mesdames. Maria Theresa herself had unwittingly advised this: 'The Princesses are full of virtue and talent; this is very fortunate for you. I hope you will deserve their friendship.' Mercy knew better: the ground floor apartments of Mesdames were a hot bed of intrigue and gossip and their influence soon became disastrous. 'I have unfortunately learned', wrote Mercy, 'that of all the ideas which Madame Adelaide continues to teach Madame la Dauphine there is not one which is not false or prejudicial to her Imperial Highness.'

It was the Dauphin, however, and not Madame Adelaide who first revealed to Marie Antoinette what precisely were the 'amusements' of Madame du Barry and the King. She wrote indignantly to her mother: 'It is pitiful to see the King's partiality for Madame

41

du Barry who is the most stupid and impertinent creature you can imagine.' Fearing her mother's reaction, she added: 'You can be well assured that I shall commit no fault either for her or against her.' Many reasons have been suggested to account for the extreme harshness of Marie Antoinette's later attitude towards Madame du Barry, but it was only after the fall of Choiseul that she began an open war of silence towards her grandfather's mistress. Up to then she had been contemptuously civil. 'She was on two occasions

Madame Adelaide, the most influential of the Bourbon aunts who contrived to make Marie Antoinette's life a misery. The portrait is by Nattier.

Madame du Barry, dressed as a milkmaid, offers Louis xv a cup of milk at Marly: a satirical engraving by Louis Lassalle.

close to me,' she wrote to the Empress, 'I did not exactly begin a conversation but I spoke to her once or twice.' All at once this polite tolerance gave way to a cutting disdain and Marie Antoinette henceforth ignored the very existence of Madame du Barry, never addressed her, never glanced her way.

Choiseul's dismissal was, as all at Versailles were aware, partly the work of Madame du Barry, who, under the advice of the Duc d'Aiguillon and the Duc de Richelieu, was determined that the hitherto all-powerful minister should pay for his contempt of her. The favourite was triumphant and soon d'Aiguillon filled Choiseul's place in the Royal Council. It was almost a foregone conclusion

43

that the Dauphine should enlist in the opposite camp when she saw the chief instigator of her marriage and promoter of the alliance publicly disgraced and dismissed from Court. Mesdames, at this period all powerful with their niece, added fuel to the flames, and thus a long, dangerous struggle was entered on at Court. Behind the Dauphine as a screen, Madame Adelaide could indulge her hatred to the full and yet fear no consequences.

On 6 January 1771, Maria Theresa sent her daughter an urgent letter enjoining her 'never to forget the gratitude she owed to Choiseul' but also advising her not to 'let herself be drawn into any faction' and to 'remain completely neutral'. Mercy advised her simply to express 'a little displeasure', no more. Marie Antoinette obeyed both their wishes by completely ignoring the favourite's presence. The whole of Versailles watched the struggle with delight. Madame du Barry, according to the Duc de Croy, was a kindly creature on the whole and far from being spiteful, but being vain and silly, she could not swallow the almost daily occurring affront and complained loudly to Mercy, to d'Aiguillon, to the King himself. If the Dauphine would but address one word to her, she declared, she would be satisfied.

Maria Theresa, accustomed to give short shrift to ladies of easy virtue by having them confined to reformatories, was now forced to order her daughter to be civil to a creature of the same sort. Her language, plain to a fault, left Marie Antoinette cold. Day after day she encountered the favourite at dances, festivals and round the gaming-table, only to give her a disdainful and icy stare. The civil words which du Barry, the King, Kaunitz, Mercy and even Maria Theresa wanted, remained unspoken.

A half-grown girl was daring to flout the openly expressed wishes of the King of France. Louis XV, seriously annoyed, summoned Mercy and begged him to use his influence with the Dauphine. 'Hitherto you have been the spokesman of the Empress,' he said. 'For a little while I should like you to be good enough to act as mine.' Not slow to grasp that the affair had become one of high politics, Mercy made the strongest possible recommendations to Marie Antoinette, making her understand that a breach between Habsburg and Bourbon would shatter her mother's hard work, and the blame rest for ever on her own shoulders.

On 16 July 1771 Marie Antoinette at last gave way. She agreed to say a few words to Madame du Barry, but in Mercy's presence. She would stop, speak to Mercy and say a word 'as though by chance' to the Comtesse. On the appointed evening Marie

Antoinette told Mercy: 'I am very nervous but do not fear, I shall speak.' She was only a step away and was about to speak to the favourite when Madame Adelaide broke in abruptly 'It is time to leave! Come, we are going to wait for the King with my sister Victoire.' The Dauphine turned and fled. She had made the mistake of telling her aunts about her promise. The position was now even worse than it had been. 'Well, Monsieur de Mercy,' said Louis XV to the Ambassador, 'you don't seem to have achieved much. Apparently I must come to your aid.'

But it was Maria Theresa alone who could influence this stubborn child. Seriously alarmed at the turn affairs had taken, she had a grave political problem on her hands. A few months before, Frederick the Great and Catherine of Russia had approached Austria for the partition of Poland. Though Maria Theresa had been quick to recognise the scheme as a crime against a defence-less country, the idea had been eagerly supported by Kaunitz and her co-regent, Joseph II, who insisted that war would be inevitable if Austria did not comply. With a heavy conscience Maria Theresa gave way, excusing herself as she signed on the grounds that she had 'consented to follow the lead of others'. Apprehensive at France's reaction to a partition that she herself knew was unjust, she realized that all depended on the mood of Louis XV. It was now that she received from Mercy the alarming news from Versailles. Because Marie Antoinette would not speak the necessary

Madame Victoire, another of Marie Antoinette's interfering aunts, seen here in a portrait by Nattier.

46

Drouais's portrait of
Charles of France, brother
of the Dauphin and later
Count of Artois, with their
sister Madame Clothilde,
playing with a goat.
Clothilde married into the
royal family of Sardinia.

word to du Barry, the partition of Poland might very well lead
to war. Her daughter would have to sacrifice herself. 'Does one
word about a dress or a trifle cost you so much fuss?' asked the
Empress. Marie Antoinette was indignant: 'If you were able to
see as I do everything that happens here you would understand
that this woman and her clique will not be content with a word
and the whole thing will start again.' But for the sake of the
country which had never ceased to be a little her own, she gave
way at last, and promised Mercy to speak to Madame du Barry,
'but not at a fixed day and hour, so she can let it be known in
advance and make a triumph of it'.

On the first day of January 1772, Madame du Barry, with the
Duchesse d'Aiguillon and the Maréchale de Mirepoix, bowed
before the Dauphine. Marie Antoinette said something to the
Duchesse, then paused for a second in front of the 'creature' and
remarked: *'Il y a bien du monde aujourd'hui à Versailles'* ('There
are many people at Versailles today'). The whole palace heard of

47

it. The aunts were furious. The King wept with joy and greeted the Dauphine with 'demonstrations of tenderness'. Maria Theresa and Joseph II, in particular, were delighted. Poland could now be divided without any obstacle. Mercy had triumphed but the future Queen raised her head and declared: 'I have spoken to her once, but I am quite determined to stop there, and that woman will never hear the sound of my voice again.' She was to keep her word.

The struggle between child and courtesan had one advantage. It separated the Dauphine from her aunts. 'I was too young and thoughtless. Now I know where I stand,' she confessed. As a result she became more intimate with her husband. To her mother she wrote: 'He is much changed, and all for the better. He shows much friendship towards me and has even begun to repose confidence in me.' Mercy soon confirmed that 'the Dauphin is entirely captivated by his wife . . . she is so full of grace that she does everything well. It must be admitted that she is charming.'

The Dauphine could, of course, do nothing to remedy the 'fatal object' as Mercy called it, but she began to try to smarten up her husband. She stopped him eating so many cakes and, less successfully, tried to 'wean the young prince from his extraordinary taste for all work connected with building'. Sensitive about his failure as a bridegroom, the Dauphin had devoted himself more and more to his sports and recreations. Both Vermond and Mercy had been moved by Marie Antoinette's situation, and *un chien mops*, a pug dog, was sent from Vienna. Vermond wrote: 'Monsieur de Stahremberg thought it might be useful, which it is as the distraction of the moment, but this is succeeded by deep thought.'

On 1 July 1771, Louis Auguste came just once too often into her apartments dirty and dishevelled from hunting. Marie Antoinette gave her husband 'a lecture on this excessive liking for the hunt which spoiled his health, and on the unkempt and rough appearance resulting from this exercise'. The Dauphin tried to retreat but she pursued him and 'continued to point out, somewhat strongly, all the drawbacks of his way of life'. 'This language', Mercy continued, 'so upset Monsieur le Dauphin that he began to weep.' Faced with his tears, the girl was affected and began to weep too.

Her rebukes had some effect, for the Dauphin now seemed content to join his wife's circle. In May 1771, the Comte de Provence had married Marie-Josèphe of Savoy. 'We two, and

OPPOSITE Madame du Barry, painted by Gauthier-d'Agoty. From dubious beginnings she had risen to her present position of influence with Louis XV through her liaison with the Comte du Barry. 'There you are, my dear sister,' the latter wrote, 'at the most elevated point to which you could aspire.'

my sister and brother get on very well together,' wrote Marie Antoinette to her mother. The two families were soon joined by the Comte d'Artois who, in November 1773, married Marie-Thérèse, sister of the Comtesse de Provence. Her appearance was not spared by Mercy: 'She has a thin face, very long nose with an ugly tip, crossed eyes and a large mouth.' No one pitied the neglected wife who seemed 'to take no interest in anything and was very repellent' to everyone except the Dauphine who 'showed her every kindness' and drew her into the quartet she had formed with the Provences and the Dauphin. The Comte d'Artois was obliged to follow. When there was no public dinner, the three families took their meals together and then, unknown to the King, acted plays with Louis Auguste as the only spectator. In an *entresol* room in the Dauphin's apartments the young people had fixed up a kind of small folding stage which could be hidden in a cupboard. Provence was the most brilliant actor, Artois was graceful, Marie Antoinette passable and the two Savoyardes extremely bad. Campan, the father-in-law of Marie Antoinette's future *femme-de-chambre*, was the producer, prompter and principal actor. But one day, dressed as Crispino, he was surprised behind a door by a servant of the wardrobe, who was so frightened that he fell backwards with a loud cry. From then on the acting ceased, so afraid were they of being discovered.

'It was from the period of these diversions', Madame Campan tells us, 'that the Dauphin was seen to lose his timid childhood air and take pleasure in the Dauphine's society.' After a year's intimacy with her two brothers-in-law, Marie Antoinette cared less for them. 'I am more and more convinced', she admitted, 'that if I had to choose a husband from the three, I should prefer the one heaven has given me. Although he is awkward, he shows me every possible attention and kindness.'

Slowly, the Dauphin began to acquire self-confidence and gave evident proof of it on the day of his entry into Paris. For three years Marie Antoinette had lived at Versailles, at La Muette and at St Cloud, on the very edge of the city, but despite repeated requests had never been allowed to enter it. For three years the King turned a deaf ear. Her representations were always ignored, and Mercy thought, apparently with reason, that it was feared that the young pair would be received with too much enthusiasm. At last, on 18 May 1773, Marie Antoinette lost patience. She summoned up her courage and appealed directly to the King who, taken aback, agreed to let her fix a day for her state visit.

50

An ormolu mantel clock by R. Robin, formerly at the château of St Cloud.

Now that she had got the King's permission, her sense of mischief prompted her to make a private visit to Paris before her official appearance, which had been fixed for 8 June. In a mask and fancy dress, she drove with the Dauphin and the Comte de Provence to the Opera ball in the forbidden city only a few weeks before the *joyeuse entrée*. They appeared punctually at early Mass on the following morning, and the escapade remained undiscovered.

The eighth was a brilliant and cloudless summer day. Crowds of

51

onlookers stood two-deep on the road from Versailles to Paris, shouting and waving their hats, as the royal couple passed. At the Porte de la Conférence, the Maréchal de Brissac, governor of Paris, handed them the keys of the city. Salutes were fired from the Invalides, the Hôtel de Ville and the Bastille. Slowly the state carriage wound its way through the crowds, across the city, across the Quai de Tuileries, as far as Nôtre Dame, where they heard Mass and returned by a circular route to the Tuileries for dinner. When at last Marie Antoinette looked out from the balcony over the huge assembly, she cried out, almost in alarm: '*Mon Dieu*, how many of them there are!' Maréchal de Brissac who was standing

J. M. Moreau's illustration of an act of kindness by the Dauphine: in 1773, a wine-grower was accidentally wounded during one of the Court's hunts. Marie Antoinette stopped to tend him, and took an interest in his family until he recovered.

52

beside her, spontaneously rose to the occasion. 'Madame,' he replied, 'I hope His Highness the Dauphin will not take it amiss, but you have before you two hundred thousand persons who have all fallen in love with you.'

Her first encounter with the French people made a great impression on Marie Antoinette. Awestruck, she described the day to her mother: 'Last Tuesday, I was fêted in a way I shall never forget as long as I live. We received every imaginable honour. But that, although it was pleasant enough, was not what touched me the most, but the affection and eagerness of the poor people who, in spite of the taxes, which oppress them, were transported with joy on seeing us.' Tactfully Marie Antoinette said to her grandfather as they returned to Versailles: 'Sire, Your Majesty must be greatly loved by the Parisians for they have fêted us well.' But everyone recognized that it had been a triumph for the Dauphine in particular.

The public was seized with enthusiasm. [the Ambassador reported] Wherever she went she smiled at them and when after dinner she walked in the Tuileries gardens where there were over fifty thousand souls, people had climbed into the trees. She ordered the guards not to hold them back and several times she was cut off. There was clapping of hands and exclamations: How pretty! How charming! . . . The Dauphin, who played his part excellently, was regarded as an accessory to the fête: everyone talked of the Dauphine. This visit was of great significance in shaping public opinion.

Marie Antoinette, that day, had been made truly happy, as her first really spontaneous letter to her mother showed: 'I was the youngest and you have treated me as the eldest; my heart is filled with the most tender gratitude. My dear Maman praises me beyond my deserts for my affection. I could never repay her half what I owe her. I embrace her with all my heart.'

From now on Marie Antoinette had but one wish: to return to Paris. On 16 June, a week later, she went with her husband to the opera where she was loudly cheered, and cheered again in the following weeks at her appearances at the Comédie Française and the Théâtre des Italiens. 'All this is addressed to Madame la Dauphine,' Mercy wrote. 'One could fill volumes with the moving remarks which were made, the comments on the appearance, charm and gracious kindly air of the Archduchess.' The Ambassador was moved and totally disarmed when Marie Antoinette said to him: 'I shall make as few mistakes as I can. When I do make any I shall always admit it.' Maria Theresa knew better. She was well aware how her daughter could 'turn around and about in

Marie Antoinette as
Dauphine: a portrait by
Krantzinger, after Ducreux.
Her *joie de vivre* was a mask
for much private suffering
and disappointment.

order to reach her goal. She is compliant only when it is a question
of something which does not particularly affect her.' But Mercy
was prepared to forgive her many faults when he saw her good
effect upon the Dauphin.

From the end of 1773 he hardly left his wife. Marie Antoinette
said of him: 'Monsieur le Dauphin has been wonderful every time
he has been to Paris and, if I may say so, he has won the good
opinion of the people on account of the air of perfect understanding
between us. This is perhaps what has given rise to the rumour that
he has kissed me in public, although it is not true.' And she concluded, 'For a long time everyone has noticed his attentions to
me.' 'There is, however, no sign of pregnancy', Mercy observed,
'but one may hope every day for this longed for event.' The cause
of his failure was physical not psychological, as had been imagined,
and a normal circumcision would have ended the real pain, both
physical and mental, which frustrated his attempts. The constant
drama often brought tears to Marie Antoinette's eyes. Shy and
troubled, the Dauphin embraced her. 'Do you really love me?'
'Yes, you cannot doubt it. I love you sincerely and I respect you
even more.' 'The young prince seemed very moved by this remark,' Mercy reported. 'He tenderly caressed the Archduchess
and told her that when they returned to Versailles he would continue with his regime and hoped all would go well.' But on 18
December, when the Court had returned to Versailles, Mercy was

54

bound to report: 'By the most incredible misfortune, our hopes in that direction, instead of increasing, seem to have become more remote.'

Marie Antoinette, now aged eighteen, had no other consolation than to abandon herself to amusement. Sadness and frivolity, gaiety and bad temper followed each other with unpredictable frequency, much to the alarm of Maria Theresa who did not guess the reason. As often as she could, Marie Antoinette went to Paris. Nothing pleased her mischievous spirit more than the masked balls of the carnival in 1774. On Sunday, 30 January, just after midnight, she appeared at the Opera ball wearing a domino and black mask. In the crowd was a young foreigner, Axel Fersen, son of the Field Marshal Fersen, a member of the Royal Council of Sweden. He had been presented to the Dauphine earlier that month at her New Year's Ball. This evening, disguised, she went up to him. 'Madame la Dauphine', wrote Fersen in his diary, 'talked to me for some time before I recognised her; when at length she unmasked, everyone pressed around her and she took refuge in her box; at three o'clock I left the ball.' He was then aged eighteen, two months older than Marie Antoinette, and was making the tour of Europe for his education.

Marie Antoinette's most serious fault at this period was no more than an excessive love of pleasure. In it, she found some compensation for the strict and tedious Court duties to which she was submitted. For the moment her craving for pleasure did not go beyond the bounds of decorum. Her popularity was as great as ever. 'Paris is completely charmed by the Archduchess in a way that cannot be described,' wrote Mercy.

This was to enable Gluck, the Bavarian composer, to present *Iphigénie*, his newly completed opera, in the French capital. Vienna fully expected the Dauphine to smooth the composer's path, a challenge she readily accepted. Not only had he been her clavichord teacher as a child but even music had now been brought into politics by the factions that surrounded Madame du Barry and Marie Antoinette separately. When Madame du Barry professed to admire the Neapolitan composer Niccolo Piccini, her followers promptly supported Italian and French opera against what they termed 'the barbarian invasion'. Marie Antoinette insisted therefore that Gluck's new opera which the Court musicians had declared 'unpresentable' should be given a fair trial. Rehearsals went badly, the cast were out of their depth and Gluck flew into terrible rages. 'I am here, ladies, to put on *Iphigénie*. If you want to

Niccolo Piccini, the Italian composer whose interests the Parisian antagonists of Gluck embraced so fervently. He himself, however, had great admiration for the Bavarian. Some years after the Revolution, Piccini was briefly on the staff of the new Paris Conservatoire.

sing, so much the better; if not, do as you please! I shall go to Madame la Dauphine and say to her: "I find it impossible to get my opera performed!" Then I shall get in my carriage and take the road for Vienna.' Nothing but dread of Marie Antoinette prevented an open scandal.

On 19 April 1774, the Dauphine brought the whole Court to the opening performance. Even her husband had been forced to put in an appearance. The French audience were somewhat taken aback by the music. Since the mood of the house was unsatisfactory, Marie Antoinette loudly clapped every aria. 'The Princess seems to have formed a plot,' remarked a contemporary chronicler, and the sulky spectators clapped too 'in order to please Madame la Dauphine'. On the following day the throng was enormous and there were no more criticisms. German music took its place, thanks to Marie Antoinette. She had, in fact, little real knowledge of music, painting or literature. She possessed a certain amount of natural taste but she was unable to make independent preferences, being inclined merely to accept the prevailing fashion, showing a fleeting interest in anyone who had already secured recognition. She hardly read a book to the end and invariably tried to avoid serious conversation. For her, art was never anything more than one of the ornaments of life. She could enjoy only that which did not fatigue. She hardly noticed the presence of Mozart, her childhood acquaintance, who visited Paris a few years later. Had she shown the slightest interest, she could have turned his visit into the financial success he so badly needed. Instead, he left almost empty-handed, leaving the city his thirty-first symphony and the flute and harp concerto written for the Comte de Guines, later to prove one of Marie Antoinette's most worthless friends. But in the meantime her success in getting Gluck accepted had proved to Mercy what an important part his pupil would later be able to play: 'I see approaching the time when the great destiny of the Archduchess will be fulfilled. The King is growing old. . . .'

On 27 April 1774, Louis xv, when out hunting, suddenly felt extremely tired and, suffering from a severe headache, he returned to the Grand Trianon in the park at Versailles. During the night the doctors found he had fever and next morning, seriously alarmed, they ordered his removal to the adjoining great Palace of Versailles: 'C'est à Versailles, Sire, qu'il faut être malade' ('It is at Versailles, Sire, that you must be ill'). At ten o'clock the following evening Marie Antoinette and her husband came to the bedroom. The King's condition was worse. The room was almost

The title-page of Mozart's Six Sonatas for Pianoforte and Violin, Op. 2 (K296, 376–80), published in Vienna in 1781. Like Gluck, he had been knighted by the Pope at the age of fourteen, but the royal families who had taken an interest in the infant prodigy failed to support Mozart the adult.

in darkness as the patient's eyes were hurt by the slightest light. Suddenly a servant of the bedchamber accidentally raised a torch. The King's face appeared in full light: his forehead and cheeks were covered with little red spots. It was smallpox. He took thirteen days to die, slowly and horribly.

On 10 May, at a quarter past three in the afternoon, a lighted candle in one of the windows of the royal bedroom was put out. The traditional cry went up: 'The King is dead! Long live the King!'

Marie Antoinette was in her apartments. The Dauphin was there, striding up and down the room. Suddenly, in the words of a witness, 'a terrible noise exactly like that of thunder' was heard. It was the sound of courtiers running through the Hall of Mirrors to acclaim their new King. The first comers to the room saw the young Queen of eighteen and the King, a year older, on their knees, weeping bitterly. 'Oh, God protect us,' they cried, 'we are too young to reign.'

3 'Little Queen,

have a care' 1775-80

ONLY MADAME DU BARRY wept with any emotion. That evening she was made a prisoner of the state and taken to the Abbey of Pont-aux-Dames. As a last privilege the dead King's body was transferred to St Denis in the middle of the night at full gallop, but along the route the inns were full of disrespectful merrymakers who drunkenly imitated the King's hunting cries as the coach passed by. The Court went into mourning if only for the sake of etiquette: there was only optimism at the older King's death. Someone full of hope for the new reign had written 'Resurrexit' ('He has risen') on the statue of Henry IV, and Louis Auguste and Marie Antoinette were greeted with wild enthusiasm. The eighteen-year-old Queen, of whom Horace Walpole wrote: 'Hebes and Floras, Helens and Graces are streetwalkers to her', had already won respect by refusing to touch the *droit de ceinture*, 'an additional tax raised after joyful events' and levied in Paris on wine and coal.

Proudly she had assumed the crown and having recovered from her first anxiety, she was now dazzled by her new position. 'Although God caused me to be born into the rank I now occupy today,' she wrote to her mother, 'I cannot help thanking Fate which has chosen me, the youngest of your children, for the most beautiful kingdom in Europe.' But Maria Theresa was full of apprehension. Eight days after Louis XV's death she wrote to the new rulers: 'You are both very young and your burden is a heavy one. I am distressed, truly distressed by it.' To her son Joseph II, the Empress was downcast: 'I am very sorry that the King and Queen are such novices; six years more would have been better for them. I fear this is the end of your sister's peaceful and happy days.'

Maria Theresa's fears were all too soon justified. Marie Antoinette did not even wait to return to Versailles before she began to ride over its customs with careless abandon. After a short stay at Choisy the new Court went to La Muette where Marie Antoinette received the 'mourning respects'. The ceremony was long and the sombre proceedings held little that was cheerful or amusing. One of the young ladies of the palace, the Marquise de Clermont-Tonnerre, declared she was tired and sat down on the floor, hiding behind a screen formed by the dresses of the Queen and her ladies-of-honour. This should have been enough to have her sent away from Court but Marie Antoinette said nothing and, when the Marquise began to play 'all sorts of pranks', she was unable to keep a straight face. According to Madame Campan, she 'put her fan to her face to conceal an involuntary smile' but

PREVIOUS PAGES Versailles: the *Entrée du Tapis Vert* by H. Robert. Here Marie Antoinette could escape from the rigours of Court life, and Robert's painting shows her in the foreground.

less kind witnesses declare that 'The Queen most improperly burst out laughing in the faces of the sexagenarian duchesses and princesses who had thought it their duty to appear at the ceremony.'

The following day certain ladies announced that they would never again set foot in the Court of 'this mocking little thing'. Marie Antoinette shrugged her shoulders and called them 'strait-laced', '*collet montés*', a nickname of her own invention. In the same way, she described as 'centenarians' ladies who were not necessarily old. 'When one has passed thirty', she remarked, 'I cannot understand how one dares to appear at Court.' Remarks in this vein were not likely to endear her to their victims. Worse still, she had slighted the Duchesse d'Aiguillon during those mourning respects. When the Duchesse made her bow, Marie Antoinette did not speak to her and 'looked down her nose contemptuously'. On the next day the d'Aiguillon clique, formerly the coterie of Madame du Barry, was singing:

> *Petite reine de vingt ans*
> *vous qui traitez si mal le gens*
> *vous repasserez la barrière.*
> [Little queen of twenty years,
> Who treats the people so badly,
> You will cross the frontier again.]

Marie Antoinette was unaware of the censure. She had been reigning for only a month.

The inlaid top of a writing desk, part of a mechanical table made for Marie Antoinette in 1776.

61

Roslin's portrait of the Duc
de Choiseul. Madame du
Barry's part in the dismissal
of Choiseul from Court drew
Marie Antoinette's even
greater hatred upon her.

The new reign opened with a clean sweep of the leading ministers
of Louis XV: Maupeou, d'Aiguillon and the detested Abbé Terray.
'The Abbé is laughing,' went the saying, 'Has misfortune come to
someone?' Refusing the Duke of Choiseul but simultaneously
reaching for the security of the past, the young King sent for the
seventy-three-year-old Comte de Maurepas. Two decades before,
he had been deposed by Madame de Pompadour; Louis XVI now
asked him to form a new ministry.

D'Aiguillon, his nephew, at first retained his portfolios and his
title of Chancellor. But in her intense dislike of him, the Queen was
at one with the vast majority of Frenchmen who hated this minister
with his 'yellow face and character inclined to spying and unfeel-
ingness'. She could not forget the injuries she had received as
Dauphine and daily she importuned her husband for his dismissal.
'Being unable to restrain her animosity,' wrote Mercy 'the Queen
brought about by herself the dismissal of the Duc d'Aiguillon who,
but for her, would have retained his position.' At the beginning
of June the Chancellor sent the King his double resignation.

62

D'Aiguillon's disgrace should automatically have meant the return of Choiseul as Minister of Foreign Affairs. Louis, however, though yielding to Marie Antoinette's demands that Choiseul should return to Court, refused to make him part of the new government. He confined himself to saying to the 'champion of the Alliance' when he saw him on 15 June, 'You have lost a lot of hair since I last saw you, Monsieur le Duc.' Maria Theresa was satisfied by this partial success for she did not wish Choiseul's return to power. 'In the present state of affairs a minister of Choiseul's character would not suit us,' she informed Mercy.

Marie Antoinette, therefore, had to be content with the dismissal of d'Aiguillon but, in a letter to Count Rosenberg, who had just returned to Vienna from Versailles, she could not resist describing how she had tricked the King into seeing Choiseul: 'You will never imagine how cleverly I managed it. I told him I had a fancy to see Monsieur de Choiseul but could not quite decide on the day. I did it so well the poor man arranged the most convenient hour for me to see the Duke,' and fell into the trap by 'happening' to meet Choiseul when he came. The Viennese courtier, shocked at the way she described the King as '*le pauvre homme*', showed Marie Antoinette's letter to her horrified mother. 'What a manner,' she wrote hastily to Mercy, 'What a way of thinking! It confirms my worst fears. She is racing to her ruin.' Her daughter was instantly compared to a Pompadour and a du Barry in her conduct and trickery, and Joseph's first letter to his sister was so strong that the Empress had made him re-write it.

Maurepas's new colleagues were men of character and ability. Vergennes, an experienced diplomatist, was at the Foreign Office, St Germain at the War Office; the universally respected Malesherbes was Minister of the King's household and, most important of all, Turgot, the dynamic *intendant* of Limoges, was at the Treasury. At last there seemed a real prospect of national recovery. When Louis XVI and Marie Antoinette appeared in Paris in the late summer of 1774, there were still signs of enthusiasm in the streets.

Rapidly Turgot initiated reforms. Since expenditures grossly exceeded revenues, he ordered cuts in the former, a move greatly unpopular among those affected. 'What,' said the King when Turgot resisted paying a pension to someone, 'what possibly are a mere thousand *écus* a year?' 'Sire,' replied Turgot, 'they are the taxation of a village.' As an encouragement to farmers, the Finance Minister ordered freedom of the grain trade, but there was a series

Rose Bertin, the dress designer who transformed Marie Antoinette's appearance and indulged the taste for extravagance which was to be the Queen's undoing. From a shop in the Rue Honoré, the 'Grand Mogol', her business expanded into a workshop staffed by thirty-six seamstresses.

of bad harvests, the price of bread rose and there were riots even at Versailles. Louis XVI forbade firing on the rioters and ordered the price of bread reduced. The rioting continued, the order was rescinded. Turgot imported foreign wheat, and prices fell, but two rioters were hung in the Place de Grève.

The reign which had begun so well now seemed to offer less hope. Marie Antoinette too, in a few months, had squandered much of the good will, advanced with such eagerness when change was in the air. A few weeks after the change of ruler, Mercy was able to report on the prospects of the new regime. He was no longer afraid of the aunts who now lived at Bellevue, once the home of the Pompadour. 'The Queen has received Mesdames in a friendly way but has indicated that the time of their domination is over.' In the princes, on the other hand, he found a new source of anxiety. The King's dislike of his brothers was unconcealed but Marie Antoinette 'allows them too much familiarity. Her supreme position requires dignity; any appearance of equality, even in her own family, should cease.'

Something more important weighed on Marie Antoinette's mind and forced her to continual restraint: the question of etiquette. To her mother she had written joyfully: 'The King has left me the liberty of choosing the persons to fill the new positions in my house as Queen.' Among the first to go was the tiresome 'Madame l'Etiquette', but even dismissal could not eliminate the servile code which she was forced to obey. The rules of etiquette which led the French royalty to be treated in private as idols, made them in public, martyrs to decorum.

'The Queen's toilette was a masterpiece of etiquette,' wrote Madame Campan, who went on to describe it in detail:

The Mistress of the Robes handed the petticoat and presented the dress. The Lady-of-Honour poured water for washing the hands and handed the chemise. When a princess of the royal family was present, the Lady-of-Honour yielded her this latter office but did not yield it directly to princesses of the Blood. In their case the Lady-of-Honour handed the chemise to the first waiting woman who presented it to the princess of the Blood. Each of these ladies observed these customs scrupulously as they were privileges. One winter day the Queen, who was quite undressed, was about to put on her chemise. I was holding it unfolded; the Lady-of-Honour entered, hastily took off her gloves and took the chemise. There was a knock at the door, which was opened; it was the Duchesse de Chartres. She took off her gloves and came forward to take the chemise but the Lady-of-Honour would not present it to her. She gave it back to me and I gave it to the princess. Another knock: it was

64

the Comtesse de Provence; the Duchesse de Chartres handed her the chemise. The Queen held her arms across her chest and seemed to be cold. Madame noticed her discomfort and merely throwing aside her handkerchief kept on her gloves and in putting on the chemise, disarranged the hair of the Queen who began to laugh to conceal her impatience, but not without having muttered several times: 'How odious! What importunity!'

Marie Antoinette fretted in vain. At the least step she was accompanied by a small battalion. She now had over five hundred servants of her own. 'For whom is the detachment of warriors I found in the courtyard intended?' the Abbé Vermond asked her sarcastically one day. 'Is some general going out to inspect his army?' Her ladies would listen enthralled as she wistfully described to them the patriarchal manners of the House of Lorraine whose disregard for etiquette had been assimilated by the Habsburgs. She told them how the dukes of Lorraine, her ancestors, would levy their taxes by going alone to church and, standing up after the sermon, would wave their hats in the air and state the required sum.

Madame Elisabeth, sister of the Dauphin. She was with the doomed royal family right up to the bitter end. The portrait is attributed to Madame Vigée-Lebrun.

Her longing to substitute the simplicity of the Viennese habits for those of Versailles now led her to make errors which did her more harm than she could possibly have imagined. Instead of dining in public, a custom she had particularly hated when Dauphine, she now inaugurated little intimate suppers where she and the King entertained only princes and princesses of the Blood and a few intimate friends. Mesdames were dismayed, the elder courtiers shocked, but the Queen was determined and a new fashion was set. She also rid herself of being followed by two of her women in Court dress during those hours of the day when her ladies-in-waiting were not with her. From now on she was accompanied only by a single *valet-de-chambre* and two footmen.

The famous *levée* was also simplified. Once her hair was dressed, she left her ladies-in-waiting and, followed only by her women, she returned to her private rooms where, with no spectators, she could quietly get dressed and look over her wardrobe.

Up to this time the Queen had shown very plain taste in dress. It was scarcely two months after the death of Louis XV that the Duchesse de Chartres had presented Rose Bertin to the young Queen. As soon as the blue and black of the 'little mourning' ended in November 1774, Mademoiselle Bertin threw herself into what she called her 'work with Her Majesty'. Several times a week, early in the day, she would arrive at Versailles with her enormous boxes

out of which came dresses called 'indiscreet pleasures', 'stifled sighs' or 'masked desire'. One morning, as the Queen was hesitating over a new colour, the King entered. 'That's the colour of fleas!' he said contemptuously, as he looked at the brown taffeta. And so *'puce'* became fashionable, distinctions soon being drawn between *'ventre de puce'* ('flea's belly') and *'cuisse de puce'* ('flea's leg'). When, a few days later, Marie Antoinette chose an ash-blonde silk, the Comte de Provence, more gallant than his brother, declared that it was the colour of the Queen's hair. Couriers were soon sent to the Gobelins and to Lyons with a lock of her hair, thus enabling the weavers to reproduce the colour exactly.

With Léonard, the Queen's hairdresser, Rose Bertin would also design elaborate hair-styles, the *'poufs aux sentiments'* for which she was now famous. There were coiffures *'au lever de la Reine'*, *'à la puce'*, *'à l'Iphigénie'*, *'à l'Eurydice'*, *'à la modestie'* and *'à la frivolité'*. Marie Antoinette had a passion for feathers. The coiffure *'à la Minerve'* had as many as ten, which were so tall that one day she found it impossible to enter the coach to go to a ball given by the Duchesse de Chartres. 'Ornaments fit for horses,' said Mesdames spitefully from their château at Bellevue. In February 1775, when the Queen sent Maria Theresa a portrait of herself with her head covered in feathers, the Empress sent it back, pretending to imagine that there had been a mistake in the destination of the present: 'I did not see the portrait of a Queen of France but that of an actress.' Mercy pointed out that 'in this matter the Queen is merely following a fashion that has become general', but the Empress would have none of it: 'A young and pretty Queen, full of charm, has no need of all this nonsense.'

Maria Theresa was not aware of the more serious disadvantages of Marie Antoinette's craze for Rose Bertin. According to Madame Campan, 'The Queen was naturally imitated by all the other women. . . . The young ladies' expenses were enormously increased; mothers and husbands grumbled; a few scatterbrains contracted debts; there were unpleasant family scenes and coldness or quarrels in several homes. It was widely said that the Queen would ruin all the French ladies.'

But it was her own reputation that the Queen was ruining. Another drama of expenses was unfolding. Marie Antoinette had discovered a passion for jewellery and found it impossible to resist her shrewd jewellers, Böhmer and Bassenge, Jewish immigrants from Germany, who made it easy for her to buy; though unashamedly charging her double prices, they gave her long credit

68

and would always repurchase jewellery she had grown tired of, for half the purchase value. The end of 1775 saw the purchase of a pair of diamond earrings which brought Marie Antoinette seriously into debt. A little later she bought, for 250,000 *livres*, bracelets which 'loaded her with debts'. When Maria Theresa wrote that this 'filled her with anguish for the future', she replied lightheartedly: 'I would not have believed that anyone would have tried to occupy my dear mother's kind attention with such trifles.'

A further drain on the finances of the state was the gaming table. Until now, the usual game had been Lansquenet, played for moderate stakes only. But Marie Antoinette now rediscovered the notorious game of faro, the favourite hunting-ground of eighteenth-century card-sharpers. Louis XVI seemed strangely tolerant of his wife's gambling activities though he had forbidden faro elsewhere under severe penalties. Marie Antoinette even persuaded him to get someone from Paris to hold the bank at faro. 'It will not matter so long as you play for one evening,' the King conceded. The banker arrived on 30 October. The Queen and her friends played all night and into the morning. The Queen left at four o'clock but the game continued in the evening of 31 October at Madame de Lamballe's house and went on well into the morning of All Saints' Day to the scandal even of the Court. 'You allowed one gambling session without fixing its length', Marie Antoinette explained to her husband, 'so we had a perfect right to prolong it for thirty-six hours.' 'You are a worthless lot,' replied the King, annoyed, but his weak nature could do nothing to curb her passion for the card table.

Inevitably, Mercy one day found the Queen anxious and 'worried about the state of her debts, of whose total she was not herself aware'. Although the Queen's allowance had recently doubled, the ambassador found a tidy deficit of 487,727 *livres*. The Queen was 'somewhat surprised' but she showed no sign of panic.

Surrounding the Queen was an almost unbreakable circle of friends, few of whom possessed any redeeming qualities and who did not hesitate to use their friendship to further their own ambitions. The men were led by her younger brother-in-law, the Comte d'Artois, who, though treating the King with surly disrespect, paid close attention to Marie Antoinette and encouraged her 'taste for dissipation' when it seemed in danger of flagging. On 9 March 1775, Artois and his cousin the Duc de Chartres invited the Queen to preside over the first horse-races to be held in France. In his *diable*, an open two-wheeled carriage, he drove

her to the track on the outskirts of the Bois de Boulogne but significantly Marie Antoinette was very much less applauded than usual. Louis XVI, in a rare mood, ordered the stand specially built for the Queen removed. Though he connived at her gambling, he deeply disapproved of this new fashion from Newmarket.

Marie Antoinette was oblivious to the frosty reception. During this first winter of her reign she was chiefly occupied by her balls. The pages of Papillon de la Ferté, keeper of the privy purse, reflected the Queen's frequent requests 'which never cease to entail rather heavy expenses in view of the large number of plumes and fine gilding ordered by Her Majesty'. Mercy was deeply disapproving: the carnival of 1775 'gave the young people too easy an access to the Queen', he complained.

Her circle of friends was exclusive. Montfalcon, who sheltered behind the name of Comte d'Adhémar, was forgiven his dubious nobility for he was 'very fashionable' and could sing while accompanying himself on the harp. He had been presented by another of the Queen's friends, Vaudreuil, who was exquisitely polite, 'knew how to speak to women' but was apt to go into terrible rages. Esterhazy, a Hungarian officer newly arrived at the Court, had 'brutal good looks' and exigent demands. He needed his debts paid and wanted to acquire a regiment. The Queen satisfied him on both counts and even occupied herself with garrisoning his hussars. 'Why have you sent Esterhazy's regiment to Montmédy, which is a bad garrison?' she asked St Germain, the minister of war, 'See that it is sent somewhere else.' As a result the Hungarian received Rocroy, a much sought-after garrison.

Another foreigner was the Prince de Ligne, 'an Austrian in France and a Frenchman in Austria'. He adored Versailles: 'The love of pleasure first brought me here; gratitude brings me back.' He was the most disinterested of Marie Antoinette's friends. 'We adored her', he said, 'without dreaming of loving her.' The friend with most influence was Besenval, half Polish, half Swiss, who bore the rank in France of Lieutenant-Colonel of the Swiss Guards. According to him, Marie Antoinette, 'with no fund of personal gaiety', was interested only in 'the gossip of the day, little carefully versed familiarities' and 'in particular the kind of scandal heard at Court'. Besenval was past-master in this line, having, it was said, an excellent style of bad manners and 'being able to risk impertinence which suited him perfectly'. The most dangerous of them all was Lauzun. According to Mercy he was 'very dangerous on account of his restless mind and his collection of all kinds of bad

OPPOSITE Baron de Besenval: one of the circle of Marie Antoinette's intimates, he was witty and scurrilous, and had a dangerous talent for intrigue, exercised to the full on behalf of the 'Choiseul party'.

71

qualities'. But, like Besenval, he amused the Queen for he too knew how to talk the 'nonsense' which was popular in her circle.

According to Madame Campan, the Queen's friends thought of nothing but trivialities which resulted in a profound ignorance. Marie Antoinette was the best example. She never opened a book except the sort which led Joseph II to reproach her with the 'trashy reading she filled her mind with'. Maria Theresa knew that it was all the more difficult for the Queen to fix 'her attention on interesting objects', since according to Besenval, her conversation was 'inconsequent and sprightly, flitting from one thing to another'.

Underneath his role as clown, Besenval was as ambitious as the rest of the Queen's associates. In April 1775 the coterie urged the Queen to demand a marshalship for the Duc de Fitz-James. St Germain was horrified: 'No one knows anything of Monsieur de Fitz-James's actions in war!' All Paris laughed at the nomination. To mitigate this incredible promotion, the King nominated seven other marshals who were hardly better qualified. The reaction was predictable:

> Rejoice O happy French, break forth and sing!
> The marshals who have been appointed by the King
> Will bless us with eternal peace for sure
> Since not a single one is made for war!

The Queen had proved to her friends she had influence with the King. Besenval soon considered they could go further. Both he and Mercy suspected the former chancellor, now exiled a few miles from Versailles, of instigating the libels and pamphlets which were daily poured out on Marie Antoinette. Besenval, besides, belonged to the 'Choiseul party' and it suited his personal feelings to punish d'Aiguillon further. 'There was not much reason for exiling him,' wrote Besenval. 'I advised the Queen to stress his audacity in attacking the Comte de Guines.'

The Comte de Guines was French ambassador to England, though he spent more time at Versailles. Occasionally he used diplomatic privilege as a cover for his smuggling activities and, when discovered, blamed his secretary. The matter came to trial, at which he declared that the Duc d'Aiguillon was trying to ruin his reputation. Marie Antoinette jumped to the defence of de Guines and, through the intervention of the King, he was acquitted. On 30 May 1775 at Marly when the Light Horse commanded by the Duc d'Aiguillon rode past, Marie Antoinette sharply drew down the

OPPOSITE Fragonard's well-known painting *The Swing* (c. 1766). It epitomizes the philosophy of life embraced by Marie Antoinette and her friends, in which innocent diversions and entertainment came before duty.

blinds of her carriage. The ex-minister even declared that she
put her tongue out at him. That evening she insisted that the King
exile him to a further distance. 'Madame, what shall I write?'
Maurepas asked the Queen in desperation. 'Whatever you like,
but he must go!' In a few days d'Aiguillon had been relegated to
a half-ruined château in the heart of the Agenois. The sensation
caused by this summary treatment was far greater than had been
expected. Even those who had most disapproved of d'Aiguillon's
behaviour were shocked by this apparent lack of justice. Marie
Antoinette came in for the greater share of the blame. 'Her part in
the matter', wrote the Comte de Provence, 'gave her the reputation
of being bad-tempered and revengeful.'

The hope of her well-wishers was now concentrated on Louis's
coronation at Reims, which was settled for Sunday, 11 June 1775.
Very early that morning, to the delight of those who recognized
her, Marie Antoinette stood among the crowds in the streets to
watch her husband's state entry. At the coronation itself, her
evident emotion touched all present. It was a moving occasion.
'I was quite surprised to find myself in tears,' reports the Duc de
Croy, 'and to see all around one in like case; the Queen was so
overcome that her eyes were streaming and she was obliged to
wipe her tears away with her handkerchief, which increased the
general emotion.' At the end of the ceremony the doors of the
cathedral were opened, and the crowd rushed in and birds in their
hundreds, set free by fowlers, fluttered over their heads to sym-
bolize the freedom and justice which the new monarch would
bring his people. Outside, every bell in Reims was echoing the
great bell of the cathedral. 'The Queen, overcome with emotion,
was obliged to withdraw for a short time. When she reappeared
she received a similar homage to that first offered by the nation
to the King.'

She did not realize, as Mercy wrote to her mother on 23 June,
that all this was 'a momentary success which should not dazzle'
since 'there is not sufficient foundation for it'. That same year she
had been dealt a warning: at the time of the 'flour wars' the rioters
talked of going to 'shake up' the nineteen-year-old Queen.

But Marie Antoinette, once back at Versailles, resumed her life
of pleasure. The Empress, warning her against this 'endless dissipation', exclaimed: 'I cannot put it too strongly to you so as to
save you from the abyss towards which you are rushing.'

The winter of 1776 was the coldest in memory. The Queen and
her friends discovered a new delight in going by sledge along the

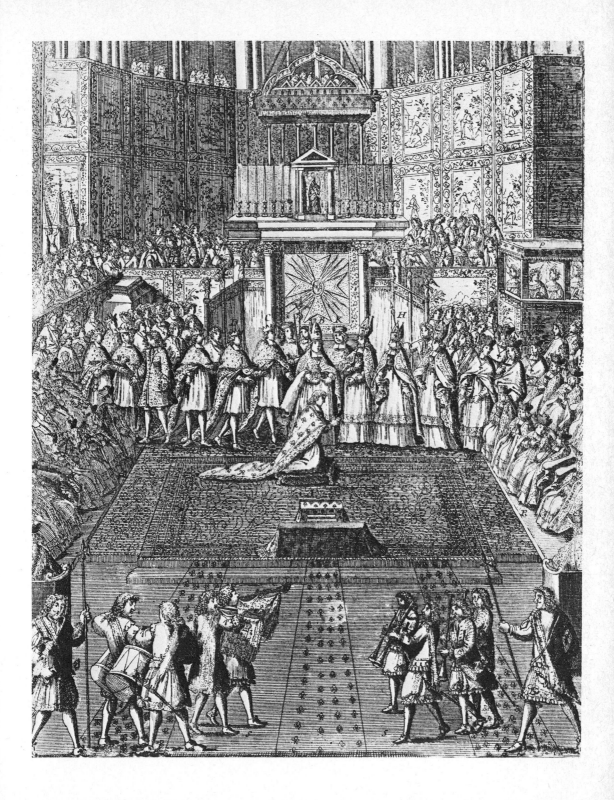

boulevards. Louis XVI put on an old overcoat and walked in the country where he paid poor people to break the ice or pardoned wood stealers arrested by the guards in the Ville d'Avray. One morning, on his return, he met Marie Antoinette as she was returning from a ball at the Opera. 'Did the public applaud you?' he asked. Sullenly, she made no reply, and Louis understood. 'Apparently, Madame, you had not enough cheers.' 'I should like to have seen you there, Sire,' she retorted, 'with your St Germain and your Turgot. I think you would have been rudely hissed.'

Marie Antoinette had never liked Turgot since he had dared to recall the Comte de Guines, that favoured member of her coterie, from the French Embassy in London. Turgot, through his far-reaching plans for reform, had succeeded in offending nearly every significant circle of power, but it was Marie Antoinette who was probably crucial in forcing the King's hand. Three times she made her husband re-write a letter according de Guines in exchange for the loss of his Embassy 'permission to bear the title of Duc'. 'The Queen's scheme', wrote Mercy, 'was to demand that the King should dismiss Turgot and even send him to the Bastille, on the same day that the Comte de Guines was declared a Duc.' Her partial responsibility for his sudden departure was equalled only by the King's weakness. In May 1776 Turgot was dismissed before he had been able to complete or submit to the King his plan for reorganizing the finances, a plan which might have saved the monarchy.

Mercy was about to discover the reason and the excuse for the irresponsibility of her behaviour both in the political field and in the 'thirst of pleasure' which had such a 'mysterious power' over the Queen. One day when the ambassador was repeating his reproaches, Marie Antoinette became 'sad and thoughtful' and with a heavy sigh 'went into a few details of the distress caused to her by her situation' as a 'married' woman. 'I must find it in increased amusements,' she told him. She could not hope to share her amusements with the King. 'My tastes are not the same as those of the King, who cares only for hunting and machinery. You must admit that I would be somewhat out of place in a forge,' she wrote to Count Rosenberg.

Louis XVI undoubtedly adored his wife but the marriage was still unconsummated. At the end of 1774 he discussed the subject with his doctor, Lassone, who strongly recommended a circumcision. As Marie Antoinette told her mother on 17 December, the King was very favourably disposed but when, a little later, the

OPPOSITE Blindman's Buff: another of Fragonard's canvases of the frivolous life of the Parisian aristocracy before the storm broke. After the Revolution he was superseded in the public favour by artists with a more serious view of life such as David, and it was David who managed to secure a job in the museums service for this forgotten painter.

surgeon showed him the gleaming instruments, he put it off once again. 'There is certainly no indifference on my side', she wrote to the Empress, 'but my dear mother must understand that mine is a difficult situation.'

To make matters worse, the Comtesse d'Artois, in 1777, gave birth to a son. Madame Campan describes the humiliation Marie Antoinette felt on this occasion, when,

The market women and fishwives, who asserted their right to crowd the palace at times of royal birth, followed the Queen to the very door of her apartments, shouting in the toughest and most vulgar terms that it was up to her and not to her sister-in-law to provide heirs to the French crown. Hurriedly the Queen closed her door on these vicious hags and closed herself in her bedroom with me to weep over her sad state.

To her mother Marie Antoinette wrote quite pathetically of the pains she suffered 'at thus seeing an heir to the throne who was not my own child'. However, she was soon herself, complaining of the 'coldness' of the King and turning more recklessly than ever to unbridled spending, borrowing, gambling and horse-racing.

The reign of the favourites was about to begin. The first of these, the Princesse de Lamballe, was, at twenty-one, already two years a widow. Her ducal husband had died of syphilis after recounting to her all the details of how he got it, a tale of debauchery from which she was never quite to recover. Pale, frail and subject to fainting, she was taken under Marie Antoinette's wing, who, for her sake, revived the sinecure post of Superintendant of the Queen's Household. Though by no means a beauty, she was said to have been 'pretty from a distance', and possessed grace and charm, apart from a loyalty to Marie Antoinette which was never to waver.

The Princess de Lamballe had only just been nominated to her new post when Mercy reported to the Empress that she 'has just been supplanted by a young Comtesse de Polignac for whom she [Marie Antoinette] has developed an affection much stronger than for any of her predecessors'. They were soon to be inseparable. To Madame de Polignac, Marie Antoinette, for the first time in her life, gave her whole heart. With her she felt absolutely at home, remarking '*J'y suis moi*' ('I am myself there'). For seven years till she succeeded the Princesse de Guéménée in 1782 as '*Gouvernante des Enfants de France*', Madame de Polignac held no official post but her influence was supreme. Marie Antoinette's exaggerated affection for her new friend set all Paris talking and at Court unleashed a drama. The astonished Mercy related that 'The two

78

favourites, mutually very jealous, are constantly complaining about each other and quarrelling.' Fontainebleau was a battlefield for these ladies who each had her own partisans, enemies, jealousies and intrigues. The pamphlets and songs increased. It was 'an epidemic', the Queen exclaimed, adding lightly: 'I was not spared. Both tastes were freely attributed to me: for women and for lovers.'

Mercy disliked the Comtesse de Polignac from the first. The Lamballe, he reported, had good qualities but was too young and inexperienced. The Polignac, a person of very little intelligence, was subject to very undesirable influences. Each possessed highly disreputable champions:

The Princesse de Lamballe is supported by the Comte d'Artois, the Duc de Chartres, and all the Palais Royal set whose intrigues fill me with alarm. The Comtesse de Polignac's partisans include Baron de Besenval, an aunt of evil reputation and other equally dangerous enemies: it would be difficult to say, which of the two parties might do the most harm.

Against a more formidable competitor, the Lamballe, with far less personality, had little chance. After a long and painful battle she accepted defeat and withdrew from Court, seeking compensation in asking and obtaining more favours which compromised the Queen, particularly in the military sphere.

What with the gambling habit at its height, and a first-class quarrel between the favourites, the Court was not a happy place. Versailles was becoming increasingly abandoned. Marie Antoinette, even as Dauphine, had resented its formality and the restrictions it imposed on her restless nature. Soon after she became Queen, Louis XVI bestowed on her the summer palace of the Petit Trianon. 'You like flowers,' the young King is supposed to have said to his wife, 'well, I have a whole bouquet to give you. It is the Petit Trianon.' Mercy, less romantically, implies that Marie Antoinette gave her husband a few strong hints beforehand.

Built by Louis XV for Madame de Pompadour, occupied by Madame du Barry, it was to become for Marie Antoinette a corner of retirement where she need no longer behave as Queen. At the Petit Trianon alone, Marie Antoinette felt emancipated from obligations whether to ceremonial or etiquette. Designed by Gabriel, it was one of the most graceful and delicate creations of early eighteenth-century French taste, a villa in the neo-classical style, well out of sight of Versailles but conveniently near. There were only seven or eight rooms in all, apart from the miniature library designed for her by Mique, the royal architect who had succeeded

80

Gabriel. Except for a few favourites tucked in rooms under the flat roof, there was no accommodation for anyone but the Queen and her servants.

She made few changes, careful to introduce nothing that should be ostentatious or too obviously expensive into rooms that were deliberately intended to give an impression of privacy and comfort. Here, carved and wooden panelling replaced the stiff marble of the more formal apartments of Versailles, soft hangings instead of stiff satin and heavy brocades. At the Petit Trianon, she alone was supreme, issuing decrees in her own name instead of that of her husband, subscribing them 'By Order of the Queen' much to the annoyance of those at Court. Here too, her servants were not in royal livery, but in her own livery of red and silver.

The King, strictly respecting the domestic privacies of his wife, would come here 'by invitation only', an agreement made only half in jest. On one occasion when he looked like outstaying his welcome, someone put the clock on an hour, and Louis went off to bed thinking it was eleven o'clock. He found life at the Petit Trianon far more agreeable than in the great palace. Stiffness and sometimes the most elementary dignity were laid aside.

On the stage of the *papier-mâché* theatre at the Trianon, completed in the summer of 1780, Marie Antoinette and her circle of friends would perform comic operas, such as *L'Anglais à Bordeaux* by Favart, *Rose et Colas* by Sedaine, or *Les Fausses Infidelités* by Berthe. Louis XVI was delighted and applauded wildly, 'particularly when the Queen performed her part of the play'. When there was no performance, they played at '*Tire en Jambe*', where they fought each other sitting astride sticks, or else played the famous '*Descampativos*', a sort of blindman's buff in reverse. The players were all covered with a large white sheet except for the one who was 'it'. Needless to say, under the acid pen of the pamphleteers, *Descampativos* became an orgy.

The famous *Hameau* ('Hamlet') a fantasy of Marie Antoinette's last years at Versailles, was not yet built. There, thatched cottages and a little mill were to shelter the families of a farmer, gardener and keeper and their picturesque livestock. Though Marie Antoinette may not have played milkmaid herself, as myth would have it, the *Hameau* was part of her love for the theatrical. Cracks were painted on the woodwork as if they were the work of time, and the outsides of the cottages were carefully weathered.

But in 1780 only the gardens of the Petit Trianon were finished. Marie Antoinette had exercised a decisive influence in their layout.

Marie Antoinette's Versailles

The Petit Trianon at Versailles, given to Marie Antoinette by
Louis XVI, became a very real retreat for her. Gabriel had designed
it for Louis XV, who had lived in it with Madame du Barry, and it
was Mique who was entrusted with plans for the gardens which
Marie Antoinette supervised with such enthusiasm and impatience.

TOP RIGHT Née's engraving of the Temple of Love in the English garden of
the Petit Trianon, seen by night.
BOTTOM RIGHT A contemporary plan showing the layout of the Petit
Trianon and its garden.

BELOW Louis XVI and Marie Antoinette with their children, affecting the
simple life in the gardens of the Trianon.

French taste was by now less sympathetic to the precision and regularity of Le Notre's horticultural geometry so evident in the gardens of Versailles. Rousseau, in *La Nouvelle Heloïse*, had demanded a 'natural park' and Marie Antoinette, echoing the contemporary atmosphere, wanted to 'create reality'. Rejecting the 'turco-chinoiserie' of Antoine Richard and the artificial ruins advocated by Gabriel, she settled on the plan conceived by the Comte de Caraman. The former Lieutenant-General of Louis xv's armies proposed the '*Montagne de l'Escargot*' ('snail's mountain'), an uncultivated hillock covered with yews and box, a grotto and a waterfall, also a 'Swiss' rock and a belvedere surmounted by a pavilion mirrored in a lake. The lake fed a river which flowed through the garden and after winding round a Temple of Love died away in two branches in front of the château. Everything had to be constructed in record time, 'for you know your mistress', a report of the Archives reads, 'she wishes to enjoy her garden very soon'. In spite of the cost (353,275 livres in a single year) the garden rapidly took shape. A whole forest was transported from the royal nurseries of La Rochette, near Melun, to Versailles.

Seduced by the informality of life at the Petit Trianon where 'one could breath the air of happiness and freedom', Marie Antoinette found it increasingly hard to return to Versailles. Forsaken in the intervals, it was rapidly becoming a less attractive place to visit. The French nobility, according to the Duc de Levis,

coming to realize that it was foolish to make a long journey merely in order to secure an ungracious reception, preferred to stay at home. . . . Versailles, a scene of such magnificence in the days of Louis xiv when all Europe was eager to come thither for lessons in good taste and good manners, now became nothing more than a minor provincial town, which one visited with nonchalance and left with alacrity.

Both King and Queen were withdrawing into their private worlds: Marie Antoinette to her 'Little Vienna', as those who were excluded called it, and Louis xvi to the palace attic. Under the roof were his locksmith-shop and forge where he worked regularly with François Gamin, his chief locksmith. In vain Maria Theresa lectured her daughter on the necessity of putting up with the tedious and futile duties of a representative position. 'I have one consolation', she wrote to her frivolous daughter, 'that the Emperor is coming to France and that you will profit by his advice.'

On 19 April 1777, the Emperor's sedan chair arrived at Versailles. His journey had a three-fold aim: to bully the King into fulfilling

OPPOSITE Louis XVI painted by Duplessis. Despite his noble Bourbon features, he much preferred outdoor pursuits and manual work to the exigencies of Court life.

evening, Marie Antoinette would walk arm in arm with one of her sisters-in-law or her ladies. That these and many other habits were embellished, was obvious from the libellous collections of songs against the Queen which was one day thrown into the Oeil de Bœuf. 'How many times', wrote the author of the pamphlet *A Reprimand to the Queen*, 'have you left the nuptial bed and the caresses of your husband to abandon yourself to bacchantes or satyrs and to become one with them through their brutal pleasures.' Joseph II scolded from Vienna but the Queen 'brushed it aside and replied merely by evasions which seemed like jesting'.

The Emperor, however, had more success with his brother-in-law. In July 1777 Louis XVI finally made up his mind to have the operation which he had been avoiding so long. On 30 August Marie Antoinette wrote to her mother, 'I have attained the happiness which is of the utmost importance to my whole life. More than a week ago my marriage was thoroughly consummated.' Nearly a year later Marie Antoinette (now aged twenty-two) appeared before her husband. With an expression of mock annoy- ance she announced to him: 'I have come, Sire, to complain of one of your subjects who has been so audacious as to kick me in the belly.'

In the months before the birth of her first child, Marie Antoinette found herself drawn again into the field of international politics. When Maximillian Joseph, Elector of Bavaria, had died on 30 December 1777, her first fear had been that the Emperor would be 'up to his tricks'. She was not mistaken. Joseph saw in this event a long-awaited opportunity to seize Bavaria. The support of France was vital to discourage Prussia from coming to the aid of Bavaria. But France, who had been openly aiding the rebels in the American colonies, was on the brink of war with England. When Marie Antoinette, acting on promptings from Vienna, ap- proached Louis, he replied unexpectedly: 'Your relations' ambi- tions will upset everything. They began with Poland and now Bavaria will be the second chapter.' He told her in no uncertain terms that France was strongly opposed to the Emperor's Bavarian ambitions.

But Marie Antoinette, after urgent and almost daily warnings from Mercy, was eventually forced to try her influence with Maurepas and Vergennes. The outcome was that France, though refusing to condone the swallowing of Bavaria, would be prepared to fight alongside the Empire against the Prussians if they attacked Austrian soldiers stationed in the Low Countries. Marie Antoinette

OPPOSITE One of Madame Vigée-Lebrun's many portraits of Marie Antoinette. The official portrait painter to the Queen, she went into voluntary exile at the time of the Revolution.

89

had achieved partial success, but her support of Joseph's foreign schemes was becoming increasingly half-hearted.

In giving birth to her first child, Marie Antoinette was once more to be victim to the tyranny of etiquette. As the day drew nearer, the peers started to converge on Versailles for by custom they had the right to be present in the room at the moment of birth.

On 19 December 1778 over fifty of them had crowded into Marie Antoinette's room, some in armchairs round the bed, others standing on the furniture to get a better view, all waiting and watching. It was impossible to move. The King had taken the precaution of having the enormous tapestry screens round the Queen's bed fastened with cords in case they should fall on her.

At 11.30 she gave birth to a daughter. There was a moment of panic when the blood rushed to her head and she seemed on the point of death. 'Air, warm water,' cried the *accoucheur*, 'she must be bled in the foot.' The windows were high up and had been stuck down their entire length with bands of paper to keep out the cold. The King 'opened them with such force that can have been derived only from his affection for the Queen', and soon she opened her eyes. The moment of danger had passed. All France celebrated; bells rang, guns fired in salute, bonfires were lit. That same afternoon the child was baptized Marie Thérèse Charlotte, Madame Royale.

Seven weeks later, when Marie Antoinette went to Notre Dame in Paris to be churched, she was coldly received by the crowds. Mercy was forced once more to explain to her that 'Her idea of dissipation and the expense she caused, and finally the appearance of an excessive love of amusement in a time of calamity and war might combine to estrange people's minds and required a little tact.' The only person who might still have saved her was shortly to die. In November 1780, Maria Theresa became ill from a lung infection and on the 29th of that month, died in the arms of her eldest son.

OPPOSITE Gauthier-d'Agoty's portrait of Marie Antoinette playing the harp. Though she was not particularly musical, the arrival of Gluck in Paris had encouraged her to play her 'dear harp' and to sing again. D'Agoty's painting also gives a good impression of Marie Antoinette's apartments.

4 The Circle

# of Deception 1780-5

IT TOOK A WEEK before the news of Maria Theresa's death reached Versailles. Sullen though she had been in the face of her mother's constant criticism, Marie Antoinette was for a long time to be inconsolable. Over the last four years her popularity had slowly diminished. The combination of her extravagance at Court and loyalty to Vienna had stirred up a growing resentment. Necker, a Swiss banker with a reputation for brilliance, had succeeded Turgot as Comptroller General, but he too found the same difficulties when he sought to limit the Queen's spending.

Abroad, Louis XVI and Vergennes found themselves with contradictory obligations. The British colonies in North America, in revolt against their mother country, had called upon French help, and from then on the principles of independence voiced from 1775 had caught the French imagination. Even before France had taken part in the hostilities a number of the Queen's close friends had enlisted in the American forces. Louis XVI, Vergennes and French public opinion had little inclination therefore to be indulgent towards Austria's ambitious schemes of aggrandizement. They risked being drawn only into another exhausting Continental war. Marie Antoinette, bullied by her family to defend their interests, did so with energy, sometimes with violence, always a little clumsily. Though she was to have little influence, the stand she was forced to take made her increasingly unpopular. In Europe France succeeded in remaining neutral and helping the cause of peace, but at sea, her support of the American Revolution was considerable and the presence of French troops was crucial in bringing about the capitulation of a considerable British army at Yorktown on 19 October 1781.

In 1781 Marie Antoinette, aged twenty-five, was expecting her second child.

She was then at the height of her youth and beauty [wrote Madame Vigée-Lebrun who had watched her for many hours as she painted]. Marie Antoinette was tall, beautifully made, rather plump, but not too much so. Her arms were superb, her hands small and perfectly shaped and her feet charming. She walked better than any woman in France, holding her head high with a majesty which made one recognize the sovereign among all her Court. . . . Her features were not regular. She had inherited from her family the long, narrow oval peculiar to the Austrians. But what was most remarkable on her face was the radiance of her complexion. I have never seen any so brilliant . . . her skin was so transparent that it held no shadows. For this reason I could never reproduce it as I wished.

PREVIOUS PAGES An engraving showing the preparations for the banquet given by the city of Paris on 21 January 1782, in honour of the birth of the long-awaited Dauphin.

94

Her page the Baron de Tilly, who did not like her, left the following description:

She had eyes which were not beautiful but could assume every expression. Kindness or dislike were mirrored in this look more strikingly than I have ever seen elsewhere. I am not sure that her nose matched the rest of her face. Her mouth was decidedly unattractive . . . her skin was admirable and so were her shoulders and neck. Her bosom seemed rather too full and her waist might have been more elegant – I have never seen such beautiful arms and hands. She had two ways of walking, one decided, rather hurried and always noble; the other more relaxed and swaying, I would almost say caressing, but without provoking any loss

Couder's painting of the siege of Yorktown, which took place in the autumn of 1781. On 19 October, French and American troops captured this Virginian base. Some Frenchmen felt that the Revolution in America in some respects mirrored their own situation, and Alexis de Tocqueville wrote major works on both countries' political systems.

of respect. No one ever curtsied with so much grace, saluting ten people in the single bend and giving each his due in look and inclination of the head. Just as one offers a chair to other women, one would almost always have been inclined to draw up her throne.

In the stress of the war and the 'economies', the Court had lost much of its old gaiety. Joseph II, returning to Versailles in the summer of 1781, 'found much improvement'. Marie Antoinette was determined to impress her brother by her reformed simplicity. 'When their Majesties went together from Versailles to Trianon they rode in a berlin coupé drawn by four horses without pages, guards or suite. The Queen was dressed in a muslin coat with a blue sash and her hair tied with a simple ribbon, no rouge and no diamonds.' When he left a week later, Marie Antoinette buried her head in a hat to hide her tears.

She was soon to give birth to her second child. Early on the morning of 22 October the galleries of Versailles were filling. By noon the passages and halls were full of gathering crowds, and the staircase, which made the royal life at Versailles a thing of the open air, was already crammed. But this time custom was disdained and the doors of the Queen's bedroom were shut fast. Inside, she had air and no throng of people such as had nearly killed her three years before, but outside the rejected public were never to forget this loss of privilege.

Louis XVI, in the whole of his lifetime, wrote only two narratives in his diary. That evening he was to fill two pages. (The only other time had been at the birth of Madame Royale.)

The Queen had a very good night from 21–22 October. She had a few small pains when she woke but they did not prevent her from taking a bath. She left it at half-past 10. The pains continued slight. I gave orders for the shoot I was to have held at Saclé only at midday. Between noon and half-past the pains increased. She lay down on her delivery bed and at exactly a quarter-past one by my watch she was successfully delivered of a boy.

Far more evocative than this dry account is an extract from a letter written by Monsieur de Stedingk, Fersen's friend, to King Gustavus of Sweden: 'After a quarter hour's suspense one of the Queen's women, all dishevelled and excited, entered and cried, "A Dauphin! But you must not mention it yet."' Caught by the general excitement, he rushed out of the apartment and called out to the first woman he met: 'A Dauphin, Madame! What happiness.'

OPPOSITE Marie Antoinette, dressed in the splendour, including an elaborate *coiffure*, for which she was renowned. The portrait is by Madame Vigée-Lebrun.

The woman happened to be the Comtesse de Provence whose anger and disbelief were only too apparent.

He went on to describe the scene in the Queen's antechamber:

Everyone's joy was at its height and all heads were turned. People who hardly knew each other laughed and wept by turns. Men and women fell on each other's necks and even those who cared least for the Queen were carried away by the general rejoicing.

At first no one had dared tell the Queen it was a Dauphin for fear of arousing too strong an emotion. Everyone round her held in their feelings so well that the Queen, seeing only constraint around her, thought it was a daughter. She said, 'You see how reasonable I am. I have asked no questions.'

Seeing her anxiety, the King thought it was time to reassure her. With tears in his eyes he said: 'M. le Dauphin begs to enter.' They brought her the child and those who witnessed the scene say they have never seen anything so touching. She said to Madame de Guéménée who took the child, 'Take him, he belongs to the State, but I now take back my daughter.'

One hundred and one guns thundered as a salute and one by one the guilds sent delegations to Versailles, each carrying the tools of its trade. The butchers came with their fattest ox, the pastry-makers with their richest pastry; the locksmiths brought a lock out of which sprang the figure of a tiny Dauphin when opened, and the grave-diggers brought a little coffin.

The autumn of 1781 was an eventful one. The royal couple, now certain of ensuring the continuity of the dynasty, enjoyed also the prestige of having wiped out the humiliating overseas defeats of Louis XV by the war in America. The death of the aged Maurepas in November 1781 further enhanced the position of Louis XVI who now proposed to exercise fuller administrative power himself.

Marie Antoinette, by producing an heir to the throne, had earned unlimited goodwill. It was true that her reputation was to a certain extent fixed in public opinion, that she was foreign, extravagant and bound to favourites. But, had she now taken a decisive step, from Trianon back to Versailles, out of her giddy entourage and back to the old nobility, she might, with very little trouble, have continued to hold their affection.

But after her confinement she continued without scandal, and yet at a fast-rising rate of expenditure, the habits which now seemed permanently hers: fashions in dress continually changing, cards in the small hours and performances at her private theatre at Trianon. She was still fond of balls but considered that at the

The birth of the Dauphin on 22 October 1781: an engraving by Boulogne from a songsheet.

A coffee cup and saucer, handpainted by Denis Levé, one of three made in 1781 to commemorate the birth of the Dauphin.

age of twenty-six she ought not to dance as much as she used. In three years she would allow herself no more than a quadrille or a *colonne anglaise* in an evening. When the King was present, etiquette required him to dance without ever turning his back on his wife. Hampered by this acrobatic feat, he was sometimes overtaken by the music, 'But then,' Horace Walpole declared gallantly, 'it is wrong to dance in time.' The Queen's page remembered that 'Once Louis XVI had left one could laugh and enjoy oneself.'

At the beginning of 1782, Versailles and Trianon were enlivened by new festivities. The dwarfish son of Catherine the Great, the future Tsar Paul I, with his wife, visited Versailles, sheltering in the anonymity of the 'Comte and Comtesse du Nord'. Pausing in Lyons, he overheard some ladies exclaim: 'How ugly he is!' 'At last,' he said, 'a country that does not flatter me. I would be happy to remain here.' To Marie Antoinette he spent long hours confiding his horror of Court life at St Petersburg and his mother's nymphomania. Marie Antoinette, though aware of Catherine the Great's dislike of her, gave a very courteous reception to 'those Norths' as she called them and put herself out to entertain them lavishly at Trianon.

At the end of the summer a change in the Queen's household had to be made. Monsieur de Guéménée suddenly went bankrupt for the astronomical sum of thirty-three million francs, and his wife, governess to the royal children, felt it her duty to resign. Besenval, playing upon the Queen's weakness and pride, pressed her to nominate Madame de Polignac as her successor. She gave in, although by that time relations were somewhat strained. Madame de Polignac had succeeded in exasperating even her friend by her rapacious demands. The Polignac family revenues were increased still further and Joseph II, though he had disapproved of Madame de Guéménée, declared himself 'shocked' by this choice. Marie Antoinette was to blame for the appointment, but she consoled herself by saying that she would have 'the opportunity to supervise her children's education, in particular that of her daughter, without the risk of wounding the governess's vanity'.

Twice more she was to become a mother. In 1785 she gave birth to a second son, the future Louis XVII, a vigorous and healthy boy who was given the title of Duc de Normandie. The year after, a daughter was born, the delicate Sophie Beatrix who lived only eleven months.

With motherhood began the first transformation in Marie Antoinette, or at least the beginnings of a decisive one. Emotions

Madame Viğée-Lebrun's portrait of the Comtesse de Polignac. Marie Antoinette found the Countess's sincerity appealing, but Mercy wrote of her grasping relatives: 'Almost unexampled is it that in so short a time the royal favour should have brought such overwhelming advantages to a family.'

till now squandered, at last found a normal outlet. She began to find it more agreeable to play with her children than to spend time in the diversions she had hitherto substituted. The little Marie-Thérèse, Madame Royale, never left her mother's rooms, and every 'important and serious business', as Mercy wrote to Joseph II on 28 December 1782, 'is interrupted by the little incidents of this royal child's games, and this inconvenience so chimes with the Queen's natural disposition to be superficial and inattentive that she hardly listens to what is said to her and understands even less! . . . consequently I find myself kept even more at arm's length than ever'.

101

Madame Royale and the Dauphin, seen here in an engraving by Blet after Madame Vigée-Lebrun's portrait. The children were everything to Marie Antoinette.

Mercy was soon to involve her once more in the Habsburg foreign ambitions. During the winter of 1784-5 a possible war with the Low Countries was imminent. Since 1460 the Netherlands had been in possession of the mouths of the Scheldt and they kept the estuary closed, much to the fury of the Emperor Joseph who wanted an outlet to the North Sea for his Austrian Empire. Louis XVI and Vergennes, having been at peace with England for a year, knew perfectly well that this would antagonize both London and Berlin. When, on 1 September 1784, Marie Antoinette, at Mercy's instigation, brought up the question with Vergennes, the minister clearly implied that France would not countenance such aggression. Joseph II then sent a brigantine up the Scheldt. The Dutch fired on it, and eighty thousand Austrian soldiers prepared to march. The Dutch asked for French aid and the situation started to deteriorate. Marie Antoinette's attempts to push Austria's claim were half-hearted and unsuccessful. The stormy incident eventually came to an end with the Dutch apologizing for firing on the brigan-

102

tine and having to pay an indemnity. France, which had nothing to do with the firing, promised to pay a share.

Paris immediately assumed that France's disgraceful attitude in the affair of the Netherlands and the tithe paid to the Emperor were both the Queen's doing. From now on she was known as 'The Austrian', a nickname she was to keep right up to the scaffold. This was also the beginning of the legend of cases of gold crossing the frontier and of the famous two-hundred million sent by Marie Antoinette to her brother to enable him to make war against the Turks.

In the ever-worsening financial situation the appointment of Calonne in 1783 as Comptroller-General of Finances had hardly been expedient. As a friend of Vaudreuil, the Comte d'Artois and the Duchesse de Polignac, and lover, it was said, of Madame Vigée-Lebrun, there had been strong claims on Marie Antoinette's patronage. The choice of Calonne, to all appearances excellent, proved, under difficult circumstances, to be deplorable. To revive confidence and credit, he at first embarked on lavish expenditure before, having run out of expedients, he discovered too late that the country's salvation lay in the political and fiscal measures advocated ten years earlier by Turgot. The Queen's close intimacy with Madame de Polignac had suffered from Calonne's appointment. She went so far as to say in front of her that the finances of France seemed to pass alternately from the hands of an honest man without talents into those of a skilful knave. To Madame Campan the Queen was full of remorse: 'That man will complete the ruin of the national finances. It is said that I placed him in his position.' In the meantime verses were circulating around Paris describing the Queen and her favourite digging at pleasure into the coffers of the Comptroller-General.

Part of Calonne's attempt to restore confidence in the finances of the State had been to buy the château of St Cloud for the Queen for the attractive sum of six million. As at Trianon, the Queen's livery at the door of the palace where all expected to see that of the King, and the words 'By order of the Queen' at the head of the printed papers pasted near the iron gates caused a sensation that damaged her reputation even further. 'My name is not out of place in gardens belonging to myself,' said Marie Antoinette defiantly. But in Paris, Monsieur de Esprémenil, a councillor, exclaimed in Parliament: 'It is both impolitic and immoral for palaces to belong to a Queen of France.'

The flood of pamphlets increased. Jokes circulated about her

103

Comte Axel Fersen, the Swedish soldier with whom Marie Antoinette had an enduring relationship, and who was loyal to the end. This contemporary miniature shows him at the age of twenty-eight.

relationships with Madame de Lamballe and Madame de Polignac, while others informed Louis XVI that if he wanted to see a cuckold, a whore and a bastard, he only had to look at his mirror, his wife and his son. Marie Antoinette began to find scandal sheets folded into her table napkin at mealtimes; others found themselves on to the King's writing-desk.

In all this, there was one name that was never mentioned and never coupled with that of the Queen: Count Fersen. Fersen, in his diary, had little to record about his first meeting with Marie Antoinette: 'I went to the ball given by Madame la Dauphine, which as usual began at five o'clock and ended at about half-past nine when I at once returned to Paris.' That had been in the New Year of 1774. Later that month he had talked to the masked Dauphine at a ball held at the Opera House. Such casual meetings had been frequent during the following weeks. A letter from the Comte de Creutz to Gustavus III reported: 'The young Comte de Fersen has been extremely well received by the royal family. His conduct has been absolutely discreet and decorous. With his handsome face and charming manner he was almost bound to succeed in society and he certainly has done so.'

Fair-haired, with clear blue eyes and regular features, he was, according to Madame de Boigne, 'beautiful as an angel'. The less ecstatic Duc de Lévis says: 'His face and his manner were those of the hero of a novel, not however of a *French* novel.' Cold at

A beautifully decorated harpsichord of the period (1786).

ABOVE A fashion engraving by Dupin after Watteau. The model, dressed *à l'anglaise*, her hair falling in curls at her neck, is amusing herself in the absence of her lover by shutting the bird in the cage.

RIGHT Voysard's engraving from a drawing by Desrais: in this plate the model is taking her dog for a walk, carrying a parasol and wearing a hat in the English style.

Jolie Femme en deshabillé galant, coëffée d'un Chapeau à l'Angloise, tenant un parasol à canne, et se promenant avec son chien.

first, 'circumspect in men's society and reserved with women', grave without being dull, Fersen, the Duc adds, was fond of serious conversation in which he displayed 'more sense than wit'.

One afternoon towards the end of June 1783 Marie Antoinette was playing the harp in her gilded drawing-room when Fersen entered the room. It was three years since she had seen him. In the meantime he had paid court to several ladies and even dallied with the idea of marriage to Miss Catherine Leijel, a young English lady, then to Mademoiselle Necker, the Swiss banker's rich, intelligent daughter. Miss Leijel married and Mademoiselle Necker would become the Baronne de Staël. Fersen's affections, if not his interests, were elsewhere. 'I am really glad that Miss Leijel is married', he wrote to his sister Sophia, 'I have decided never to marry. . . . I cannot belong to the one woman to whom I should like to belong and who alone truly loves me, so I will belong to no other.'

To keep Fersen close to her, Marie Antoinette now arranged the purchase of a French regiment, the Royal Suedois, for him to command. A miscarriage of the Queen, a long trip through Germany and Italy with his King, interrupted their intimacy. Then, on 7 June 1784, on the way back to Sweden, Fersen and an incognito Gustavus III stopped off at Versailles. Louis XVI, hunting at Rambouillet, was told of the visit; he rushed back and dressed so hurriedly he put on one shoe with a silver heel, the other with a red one. 'Have you been dressing for a masquerade?' the Queen asked him laughing. They stayed six weeks. 'We are in a whirl of feasts, pleasures and entertainments of every kind,' Fersen wrote to his father. Marie Antoinette seemed transformed. 'She is miraculously beautiful,' wrote the Baroness d'Oberkirch.

Fersen returned to Sweden with the royal suite, not to return to France until the birth of Marie Antoinette's second son, a son said many, of whom he was the father. When the Queen visited Paris shortly afterwards, the reception was icy. Fersen wrote sadly to King Gustavus: 'There was not a single cry of welcome but a complete silence.' On returning to Versailles she wept in Louis XVI's arms. 'What have I done to them? What have I done to them?' she asked.

Marie Antoinette soon threw herself into rehearsals for what would be, though she could not know it, her last performance in the Trianon theatre as Rosine in Beaumarchais's *Le Barbier de Seville*. There was even a fatality in her choice of comedy. With complete lack of intelligence she had deliberately chosen a play

Pierre Augustin de Beaumarchais: a portrait by Nattier. Devious and determined, he secured the performance and acclamation of his controversial *The Marriage of Figaro*. He was also one of the intermediaries through whom the French conveyed arms to the American revolutionaries.

by the author of *The Marriage of Figaro* which had been expressly forbidden by the King. From 1781-4, though accepted by the Comédie Française, it had awaited production at the royal theatre. Louis XVI, after a reading, had declared: 'It is detestable. It must never be performed! To allow it would be the same as destroying the Bastille. This man ridicules everything that should be respected in government.' To get around the King's interdiction, Beaumarchais read scenes of his play in the salons of the privileged. Vastly amused, though the humour was entirely directed against themselves, his aristocratic listeners persuaded Louis XVI to allow its production. On opening night, 27 April 1784, windows, doors

110

and even the outside railings gave way under the pressure for seats. Beaumarchais's *Figaro*, applauded by its own targets, was a wild success; its production, as Louis XVI had predicted and Napoleon later confirmed, was 'the Revolution already in action'.

Now the Queen of France in the spring of 1785 was rehearsing for *The Barber of Seville*. Vaudreuil was to play Almaviva, and Artois, the future King of France, Figaro, the mocker of aristocracy. There were rehearsals every day and the performance was fixed for 19 August.

On 12 July the Queen was at Versailles when the Court jeweller Böhmer arrived with a note from his partner, Bassenge. She was between Mass and rehearsals and she could give him only a few minutes. She read the letter after he had gone. 'I was reading in the library', writes Madame Campan, 'when the Queen came in with that letter saying that since I was so good at solving the puzzles in the *Mercure de France* I might try solving the one that fool Böhmer had just given her.' The letter read as follows: 'Madame: We are filled with happiness and venture to think that we have shown our respect and devotion to your Majesty's commands by our acceptance of your latest terms and we have real satisfaction in thinking that the most beautiful set of diamonds in existence will belong to the greatest and best of Queens.' Try as she might, Marie Antoinette could make no sense of the note. To Madame Campan she remarked that it could only be another proof of Böhmer's madness; she had no idea what he meant by complimenting her on the beauty of her diamonds. 'Then Her Majesty held the letter to the flame of a candle which was kept burning for the sealing of letters. "It is not worth keeping," she said. But she would regret having destroyed that enigmatic message.'

That 'enigmatic message' was the key to Marie Antoinette's fate and characteristically she threw it away. For this brief moment alone she was in contact with the intrigue of the Diamond Necklace, the most extraordinary scandal and confidence trick ever perpetrated.

The central figure had once been a neglected child, daughter of an impoverished nobleman and a dissolute serving maid. With her elder brother, her mother and father, Jeanne de Saint-Rémy, as a child of four, set out to walk to Paris leaving behind the debts which had been accumulating throughout the years at the family château of La Fontette. Baron de Saint-Rémy could claim descent, albeit illegitimate, from Henri II, the last Valois King of France. His ambitious wife reasoned that since Henri II was a cousin of the

first Bourbon, the Baron was thus a cousin, however distant, of Louis XVI. With such credentials he should go to Paris and obtain a pension from the King, or better still, a place at Court. The Baron died before he could press his claim. His wife took to the streets and eventually ran off with a soldier from Sardinia, leaving behind Jeanne, her brother and another infant daughter.

Jeanne took to begging as her only resource and at seven, by a stroke of luck, she was standing on the road to Passy, outside Paris, when the Marquise de Boulainvilliers drove past.

Jumping on to the footboard with her tiny sister on her back, she approached the Marquise with what seemed an incredible patter: 'Give alms to a poor orphan sprung from the blood of the Valois.' The Marquise ordered her coachman to pull up and after questioning the child exhaustively decided that her story was genuine. She took the children under her wing; when the Judge-at-Arms of the French nobility confirmed their descent from Henri II, the two sisters were given a small pension out of State funds.

Jeanne's delusions of grandeur began in earnest. One night in 1779 Jeanne, aged twenty-two, and her younger sister, bundled their possessions together and escaped over their convent wall to Bar-sur-Aube near Fontette. There she met Nicholas de la Motte, an army officer on leave, and married him a month before giving birth to twins who later died. From the first, Jeanne was deter-mined to climb. She persuaded her benefactress, the Marquise de Boulainvilliers, to gain her an introduction to the Cardinal de Rohan at his palace at Zabern. Clever as well as pretty, she was soon able to procure for her husband a captaincy in a regiment of dragoons and the settlement of his debts. They had now become three, as Rétaux de Villette, a friend from la Motte's first regiment, had joined them.

Not content to vegetate in the provinces, Jeanne decided that the Valois title was worth far more than the modest pension paid to herself and her husband's pay as cavalry officer. They were soon calling themselves Comte and Comtesse de la Motte or, when they wanted extended credit, de la Motte-Valois. To open the campaign, they rented a mansion in the Rue Neuve-Saint-Gilles in Paris. Warding off the money-lenders with stories of the huge estate to which the Countess was rightfully entitled as a descendant of the Valois, they kept open house with the funds thus obtained. When their creditors pressed for payment the Comtesse de la Motte-Valois fobbed them off by telling them she was going to Versailles to push her claim at Court.

OPPOSITE A contemporary print of the famous diamond necklace by Böhmer and Bassenge made up of flawless stones.

113

At Versailles she rented rooms for herself in the town and made Rétaux de Villette her personal secretary. Her petitions to the Court officials went unheeded so she tried the direct approach. To attract attention she staged a faint in Madame Elisabeth's ante-chamber while her husband explained with tears in his eyes that she was a destitute noblewoman overcome by starvation. Always sympathetic, Madame Elisabeth gave her two hundred francs. Since the first trick had been successful, she decided to repeat it a second and third time, so she fainted in the Comtesse d'Artois's anteroom and again in the Hall of Mirrors through which Marie Antoinette was about to pass. Unfortunately, the Queen, on whose generosity Jeanne had banked everything, was oblivious.

Baffled, the de la Mottes returned to the Rue Neuve-Saint-Gilles and continued to live far beyond their practically non-existent means. Jeanne was at her wits' end before she suddenly had the brainwave of telling everybody that she and the Queen had be-come friends. Marie Antoinette's circle being what it was, the story was quite feasible. She even showed her credulous acquaint-ances letters full of affection to 'My cousin the Comtesse de Valois', apparently written by Marie Antoinette. They were in fact forged by Rétaux de Villette.

Most credulous of all was the Cardinal de Rohan who at that time was sheltering Cagliostro, the greatest swindler of the day, under his roof. Jeanne aimed to use de Rohan as a way of reaching the Queen; de Rohan, believing her stories of friendship with Marie Antoinette, saw the Countess as a means to win back the royal favour he had lost some years before. Cagliostro and the Comtesse de la Motte-Valois were soon hand-in-glove; from him she knew that de Rohan's secret ambition was to become First Minister of France. She knew too that his major obstacle was Marie Antoinette.

Since the day he had welcomed Marie Antoinette to Strasbourg, he had served as French ambassador in Vienna, to the scandal of Maria Theresa and the delight of the more flighty Viennese social world. Hunting and womanizing came before his diplomatic and ecclesiastical duties, and the Empress could not wait to get rid of him. Marie Antoinette had inherited her mother's dislike of this worldly prelate and, after his return to France, she refused to acknowledge him. At the baptism of the Dauphin, the Queen stood on one side of the font, de Rohan on the other, without a glimmer of recognition on her part.

Now, in Jeanne, he saw an ideal advocate. 'Do you realize,

114

The protagonists of the Affair of the Diamond Necklace: LEFT Count Alessandro di Cagliostro, the Italian charlatan who played on the weaknesses and ambition of the Cardinal de Rohan. From a drawing by Bonneville. BELOW The Comtesse de la Motte-Valois whose corruption and audacity helped to ruin and discredit Marie Antoinette in the eyes of her subjects. A contemporary engraving.

Countess, that my fate as well as yours rests entirely in your hands?' She could convince the Queen of his devotion and loyalty. Appearing to be much moved, this 'intimate friend' promised to do her best. Already, in May 1784, the Countess informed de Rohan that the Queen was more favourably inclined. To show her change of mood, she would give the Cardinal a nod in a particular way. Jeanne, stationed in the Hall of Mirrors day after day, had noticed Marie Antoinette's curious mannerism of turning her head to glance through the doorway of the Oeil de Bœuf apartments as she passed. On a day arranged by Jeanne, de Rohan waited in the Oeil de Bœuf. The Queen glanced in, as was her habit, and de Rohan, in ecstasy, was convinced she had given him a nod.

All the time Jeanne was turning the confidence trick to her financial advantage. Letters, each more friendly than the last, were apparently exchanged between Marie Antoinette and the ambition-blinded Cardinal. Villette was hard at work. Never had the crooks dreamed of such success. From the Queen, de Rohan received a letter saying that she wished to make a charitable donation in secret. Since she was short of funds she asked him, as Grand Almoner of France, to lend her sixty thousand francs and send it to her by Madame de la Motte. Three months later they told him the Queen was again in want of money. The Cardinal obligingly pawned his furniture and plate to raise the money without delay.

The weeks turned into months and still the Cardinal, who expected a high ministerial post, waited for a public statement. Something had to be done to stop him getting suspicious and only a meeting with the Queen herself would do that. As in the last act of *The Marriage of Figaro*, the meeting would be a comedy of mistaken identity in a garden in the dark.

The *rendezvous* was to be in the Grove of Venus near the Trianon on a moonless night in July 1784. Since it was common knowledge that the Queen liked to walk in the park on summer evenings, the scheme did not sound too outrageous. To impersonate the Queen, Monsieur de la Motte found a twenty-three-year-old prostitute called Nicole d'Oliva whom he had picked up in the gardens of the Palais Royal. She bore a remarkable resemblance to Marie Antoinette and was, as Madame de la Motte later explained, 'exceedingly stupid'. Promising the girl a reward of fifteen hundred francs, they dressed her up in a simple *gaulle* dress and gave her a letter in a plain envelope. She was told she would have to hand it to a 'very great nobleman' who would meet her in the park.

Between eleven and twelve that night they took her to the

grounds of the Trianon. There she was given a rose and told that all she would have to say was, 'You know what this means.' De Rohan, informed by Jeanne that the Queen was waiting, hurried off to the Grove of Venus. Mademoiselle d'Oliva held out the rose saying, 'You know what this means', but forgot to hand over the letter. At that moment Jeanne ran up telling him to leave at once as the Comtesse de Provence and Comtesse d'Artois were coming. Behind the hedges, Monsieur de la Motte and Villette provided the sound of approaching footsteps. De Rohan fled, convinced that he had at last met his Queen. He was happier than he had ever been.

All this was nothing to what was to come. On the fringes of the Court circles it was known that Marie Antoinette bought jewellery in secret from Böhmer and Bassenge, the Court jewellers. They had hoped to interest her in buying a necklace which they had made twelve years before in the hope that Louis xv would buy it for Madame du Barry. The Queen, who had recently found herself in debt to her jewellers for half a million francs, refused to buy this rather ugly necklace which was made up of 540 diamonds of the highest quality. Böhmer, who had sunk all his fortune in this necklace, had even thrown himself at her feet threatening to 'go and throw himself in the river'. Sharply, Marie Antoinette had told him to stand up and not give way to these 'despairing contortions'. Böhmer could not bring himself to break up the piece and sell the stones individually. Somehow he came into contact with the Comtesse de la Motte-Valois, and, knowing her to be such a close friend of the Queen, begged her to use every influence. Jeanne saw the necklace and was dazzled. It was then that she must have had the idea of using the Cardinal to obtain it for herself.

De Rohan soon received a letter, apparently from Marie Antoinette, commissioning him to buy the necklace for the lowest price he could negotiate. Böhmer informed him that, anxious to be rid of it, he would sell it for 1,600,000 francs, a sum lower than the cost of the stones, the setting and labour. Villette forged a letter from Marie Antoinette agreeing with the arrangements he was making and enclosed her terms: 'The first instalment, in the amount of 400,000 francs, shall not be payable for six months; successive instalments of similar sums shall be payable every six months thereafter. If these conditions are accepted the necklace is to be delivered Tuesday, 1 February [1785].' Böhmer and Bassenge demanded proof that de Rohan was acting for the Queen, which Jeanne willingly provided. Villette signed the forged

OVERLEAF The château of St Cloud, painted by Martin. Here, as at Trianon, Marie Antoinette established her own Court and issued her own orders. Here, too, the royal family spent the summer of 1790 after they had left Versailles for good.

117

Louis Seize Furniture

The most significant influence on furniture design around
the middle of the eighteenth century was the discovery of
the buried sites of Herculaneum and Pompeii, which
heralded a 'return to antiquity'. Many artists and craftsmen
travelled to Rome to immerse themselves in the classical
spirit, and motifs such as the laurel leaf were incorporated
into their designs. Floral decoration on porcelain, veneers
and geometric marquetry patterns characterized the
furniture of the transitional Louis xv-Louis xvi period.

BELOW A chest of drawers with geometric marquetry work,
an oval inlaid plaque in different coloured woods, and
gilt-bronze floral decoration.

ABOVE An upholstered chair attributed to Claude,
c. 1785-95. Its legs are shaped like quivers,
with vertical fluting.

LEFT A secretaire made in 1783 by J. H. Riesener for Marie
Antoinette at the Petit Trianon. Floral decoration and
lozenge-patterned marquetry are again a feature, and the
plaque is gilt-bronze.

121

contract, 'Marie Antoinette de France'. Curiously the Cardinal did not notice the blunder; Marie Antoinette never signed any document other than by her first name, never adding 'of France'.

On 1 February the jewellers delivered the diamond necklace to the Cardinal. At dusk that evening he took it to the Countess's apartments where, in a dark little room lit only by a single candle, he waited to hand it over. After a few minutes there was a knock at the door and a voice said, 'In the name of the Queen.' Jeanne went to the door with the jewel-case and handed it to a man in the Queen's livery. He was the Queen's confidential messenger, she explained, from the Trianon. It was none other than Rétaux de Villette in disguise.

As time went on and the Queen still refrained from wearing the necklace in public, the Cardinal began to have doubts. The situation became critical as 1 August approached, the day specified for the initial payment. The Countess, in the meantime, had acted swiftly. As soon as the Cardinal had left her apartment, the necklace had been broken up. Monsieur de la Motte went over to England and in London disposed of most of the stones in Bond Street, putting the money into letters of credit.

Anxiously, de Rohan asked Madame de la Motte why the Queen did not wear the necklace. The Queen, she reported, on second thought, considered the price too high and wondered whether the Cardinal could help her by borrowing the 400,000 *livres* needed for the first payment. De Rohan sought the loan from a banker named Saint-James, who, hesitant of the whole proceedings, succeeded in stirring the Cardinal's suspicions further. Again he questioned Jeanne. This time she informed him that the Queen wanted the necklace either reduced or revalued because until then she would not wear it. De Rohan sent for the two jewellers, then and there making them write a letter thanking the Queen for purchasing their necklace. This time it was not delivered *via* Jeanne but by Böhmer himself when taking jewellery to the palace.

It was this same letter that on the morning of 12 July 1785 Marie Antoinette had read while waiting for Madame Campan to hear her lines for *The Barber of Seville*. It was the 'enigmatic message' which the Queen had carelessly held to the candle and led to the frenzy of Böhmer and Bassenge when they received no reply. Disregarding the advice of Madame de la Motte who told them to deal only with the Cardinal, Böhmer went eventually to the Queen, telling her everything he knew, with the result that all the characters involved in this fantastic intrigue were brought

122

up for trial, a trial that was to set the seal on Marie Antoinette's fate.

Napoleon was later to recognize Marie Antoinette's crowning error in the diamond necklace trial: 'The Queen was innocent and, to make sure that her innocence should be publicly recognized, she chose the Parliament of Paris for her judge. The upshot was that she was universally regarded as guilty.'

The preliminary hearings established the following: that the Cardinal really believed he was buying the necklace for the Queen, that the signature 'Marie Antoinette de France' had been forged by Villette, that the necklace had been delivered to Madame de la Motte and that her husband had sold the stones in London. The actual basis of the trial was a charge brought by Louis XVI against Cardinal de Rohan of *lèse-majesté*. At nine o'clock on the night of 31 May 1786, after a session which had lasted eighteen hours, de Rohan was acquitted on all charges by a narrow majority. A huge crowd had gathered outside the Palais de Justice and cheers went up, mixed with cries of 'Long live the Cardinal! Long live Parliament!' He had become a symbol of opposition to Marie Antoinette and all she stood for.

Monsieur de la Motte was sentenced in his absence to the galleys for life, though he never served a fraction of his sentence, Villette was banished, Nicole d'Oliva reprimanded, Cagliostro totally exonerated, but Jeanne was condemned to be flogged, branded and imprisoned in the Salpetrière for the rest of her days. There she remained until 2 June 1787 when she escaped, with outside help, to England. Once in London she poured out a non-stop flow of vitriolic and pornographic pamphlets, letters and memoirs, all directed against the Queen of France. She accused her of having ordered and received the necklace from the Cardinal, at having sacrificed her 'cousin' at the trial, of relationships with women, including herself, and a 'love affair' as Dauphine with the Prince de Rohan.

At Versailles Marie Antoinette, aged thirty and now quite alone, faced the mounting hatred that was only partly of her making.

5
'Madame Déficit' 1785-9

T HE AFFAIR OF THE NECKLACE was to become the preface to the Revolution.

> The carefree joyous days were gone, never to return [records Madame Campan]. It was farewell to those tranquil and informal holidays at her beloved Trianon; farewell forever to those brilliant fêtes and galas which served as a showcase for all the glittering splendour, the sparkling wit, the exquisite good taste of French Court life. What was more, it was farewell forever to respect and reverence for institutions of monarchy.

Slowly the country had become filled with disquiet. The bourgeoisie, enlightened by Voltaire, Rousseau and Diderot, began to question the monarchical system, and 'Le contrat social' ('The Social Contract') with its radical new ideas of liberty and the individual was given additional weight by the reports of soldiers newly returned from the American War of Independence.

If the diamond necklace trial had contributed to the general misgiving, Calonne's revelation of the deficit came as a masterpiece of ill-timing. At the end of 1786, the Comptroller-General of the finances made public the fact, hitherto concealed, that during the twelve years of Louis XVI's reign, the sum of 1,250 million *livres* had been borrowed. All fingers pointed to the Queen: henceforth she was known as 'Madame Déficit'. 'How could I have suspected that the finances were in such a bad state?' Marie Antoinette was later to ask. 'When I asked for fifty thousand *livres* I was brought one hundred thousand.' She retained her incomprehension in the face of the rising hatred directed against her. 'I shall conquer the malicious by trebling the good I have always tried to do,' she declared. Even the outward forms of reverence towards her were now disregarded. When she appeared in her box at the theatre for the first time since the trial, she was greeted with such loud hisses that henceforward she thought it best to stay away. Madame Vigée-Lebrun thought it wiser to withdraw her portrait of Marie Antoinette that was to be exhibited in the Salon, and from the Lieutenant of Police she received a warning to stay away from Paris for her own safety. In despair, Marie Antoinette, aware at last of this universal hatred, exclaimed: 'What do they want of me? . . . What harm have I done them?'

Louis XVI was obliged to dismiss Calonne and, at Marie Antoinette's suggestion, his place was taken by Loménie de Brienne, Archbishop of Toulouse. 'Make no mistake, Messieurs,' she said as she left the Council chamber, 'he is a real Prime Minister.' Those with privileges were soon to be only too aware

PREVIOUS PAGES The storming of the Bastille and the arrest of its governor, M. de Launay, on 14 July 1789. This bloody event was the real beginning of the Revolution and was celebrated as such in the years to come. An engraving by Berthault after Prieur.

126

of this. Economies had to be made at Court and for the next year he abolished 173 posts in the Queen's Household alone. Marie Antoinette cut down her style of living: Rose Bertin was dismissed, the gaming-tables disappeared, a stop was put to some additions being made to St Cloud. A number of sinecures were cancelled and more careful note was taken in respect of the public money wasted on her favourites at Trianon. Vaudreuil resigned himself to giving up his chief post as falconer; but Besenval, although he kept his Swiss Guards, was deeply wounded: 'Madame,' he said to Marie Antoinette, 'it is terrible to live in a country where one is not sure of possessing one day what one had the day before. That used to happen only in Turkey.'

In spite of the dismissal of six hundred guards and light horse, these economies did not fill the gap and Loménie de Brienne was obliged to come before the Parliament of Paris. The lawyers, however, were unco-operative and refused to register two edicts concerned with the imposition of stamp duty and a land tax, implying that the Estates General should be called. Encouraged by Marie Antoinette, Loménie de Brienne had the two edicts registered at a *Lit de Justice* held at Versailles on 6 August 1787, and the King exiled the Parliament to Troyes. The outcome was disastrous. Demonstrations were held in Paris and, with reluctance, Parliament was allowed to return to the capital.

On 19 November the conflict began again. The King issued loans for 420 million *livres* and now, for the first time, the former Duc de Chartres, now Duc d'Orleans, rose up before Louis XVI and declared the registration of the edict to be illegal.

Calonne had failed, and now de Brienne. There was only one man who might save the situation, the Swiss financier Necker. Summoned once before to try to save the financial situation, Necker had no reason to rescue these ministers of Louis XVI who previously had been only too glad to rid themselves of this Calvinist, foreigner and bourgeois. He had little reason either to love the royal family whose member, the Comte d'Artois, had once called him a 'fornicating foreign bastard'. It now fell to Marie Antoinette to coax the ruffled Swiss into helping her country once more. 'I tremble – excuse this weakness,' she wrote to Mercy on the day she summoned Necker to her private apartments, 'because it is I who have caused him to be recalled. My fate is to bring misfortune. And if he should fail like his predecessors, or if he extends the King's authority I shall be even more detested.' Necker did what he could, even lending the Treasury two million of his own money,

The Revolutionary Thinkers

In 1789 France was ripe for revolution as never before, not just because of the provocation of the extravagant life the Court led in the face of the gross poverty of the Third Estate, but also because of the climate of opinion which had been fostered by a group of brilliant philosophers who dared to challenge the authority of the all-powerful institutions of Church and State. Among these were Voltaire (François Marie Arouet), author of the *Dictionnaire Philosophique*; Jean-Jacques Rousseau, whose major work of political philosophy was *Du Contrat social*, and Denis Diderot, who masterminded the *Encyclopédie*, a sceptical work twice banned, and whose contributors included Voltaire, Montesquieu, Rousseau and Turgot.

BELOW A series of drawings of Voltaire, recording a variety of expressions: after Huber.

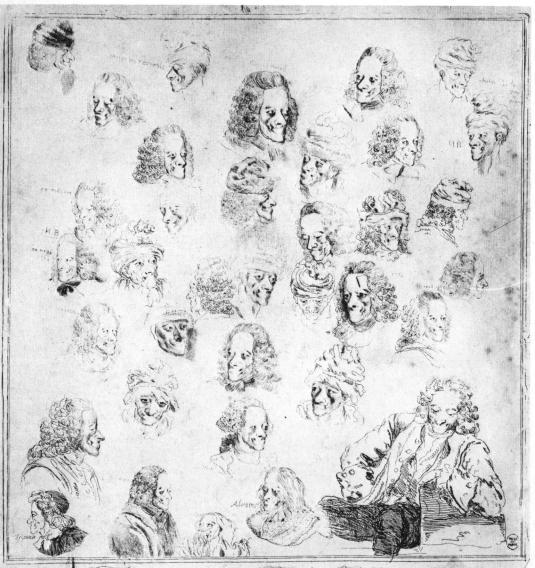

LEFT Rousseau depicted, as often, in the quiet of a country setting: an engraving after a painting by Albrier.

BELOW Wood gilding: an illustration from Vol. III of the *Encyclopédie*, which was published in thirty-five volumes between 1751 and 1776.

The recall of Necker: an allegorical engraving by Gaucher. Louis, resting his hand on a book containing Necker's works receives Necker. The crowned woman represents France, and the Latin inscription reads 'After darkness, light'.

but he too was afraid: 'I can see the great wave advancing. Will it engulf me?'

For six months before the dismissal of Loménie de Brienne on 26 August 1788 there had been one persistent cry: 'The States General and the return of Necker!' Daily, the demands for the summoning of the States General grew louder. France was beginning to align itself for the final struggle. Against Louis XVI and Marie Antoinette, and the peers and ministers still loyal to them, was the party of discontents headed by the Duc d'Orleans and the liberal thinkers gathered round him at the Palais Royal. On both sides were ranked the mass of people, no longer inarticulate.

The French legislative assembly had not been called since 1614, in the time of Louis XIII. Necker was finally to make Louis understand that they must be summoned and, at the beginning of May 1789, the nobles, the clergy and the commons, the three Estates, converged on Versailles. There were 1,165 in all, and now, for the first time, the Third Estate had as many deputies as the two others

130

combined. The winter had been severe and even now the cold was almost unbearable. Windows were covered with a thick layer of ice and even the drinking-water froze on the table. Undaunted, half Paris had flocked to Versailles to witness the scene.

At ten o'clock on the morning of 4 May, the royal train set out from the palace of Versailles to ride in state to the Church of Notre Dame where the three Estates were awaiting them. The King, in full dress, wearing a mantle of cloth-of-gold, and surrounded by the high officers of the Crown, was wildly applauded. Only a contemptuous silence acknowledged Marie Antoinette when she appeared in her violet, white and silver gown, her head surmounted by ostrich plumes. Unknown to them, her political anxieties were coupled with a great personal grief, the illness of her elder son. The Dauphin, who had now grown very thin, had a fever every evening. His vertebrae were 'displaced and projecting'. That day he had left his bed to lie on a mattress on the balcony of the Little Stable at Versailles and watch the procession of the States General going from Notre Dame to the Church of Saint-Louis.

It was a procession in which walked the last Kings of France: Louis XVI, Louis XVIII, Charles X, Louis Philippe, then Duc de Chartres, and the young Duc d'Angoulême who, one day at Rambouillet in 1830, was for three minutes to be Louis XIX of France. The Duc d'Orleans who was to send Louis XVI to the scaffold, walked with the Deputies of the Nobility, the hero of the day. In the Place d'Armes, just as Marie Antoinette was passing under the balcony where her little Dauphin was dying, a single cry greeted her: 'Long live the Duc d'Orleans!' She turned pale and was obviously near fainting when the Princesse de Lamballe hurried up. 'It is nothing . . . nothing,' she said, as she recovered her composure; but on returning to the château, she had such a violent attack of nerves that she broke her diamond bracelets.

Next day, at the formal opening of the States General, further humiliation was in store for her. Whereas the entry of the King had been greeted with loud cheers, she received only a frosty silence. '_Voilà la victime_,' whispered Mirabeau to his nearest neighbour, Gouverneur Morris, an American whose heart went out to this woman. 'The Queen wept', he was to write in his diary, 'and not a single voice was raised on her behalf. I would gladly have raised mine had I been French, but I had no standing-ground here.' It was not until the end of Necker's speech when she stood up in order to leave the hall with the King, that a few of the deputies, sorry for her 'look of sadness and depression', raised scattered

131

cries of 'Vive la Reine'. Startled by the demonstration, Marie Antoinette acknowledged it with a bow, and all of a sudden the whole audience joined in the greeting.

As soon as the parade was over, King and Queen hurried to a carriage and drove to Meudon where the six-year-old Dauphin was lying in his little bed, his condition steadily growing worse. On 3 June, the Blessed Sacrament was exposed in all the churches in Paris. At ten that evening the King left Meudon in his carriage, but Marie Antoinette never left her son's bedside. At one the following morning the child breathed his last. Etiquette did not allow the mother to weep by the little corpse which was already surrounded by twelve candles. She had to return to Versailles.

It was at Marly on 19 June that the King received 'his councils'. It was a crucial moment. Two days earlier the deputies of the Third Estate, together with a few members of the clergy, had set themselves up as a 'national assembly' as they represented 'ninety-six per cent of the nation'. Without further delay they pronounced illegal any tax raised without their consent. Necker was hastily summoned to the palace but his audience with Louis was interrupted by a message from Marie Antoinette who wished to speak to her husband in private. 'The Queen has sent for him,' murmured Necker. 'We've got nowhere.' He was quite right. When Louis XVI returned to the council room, he would have none of Necker's conciliatory scheme or plans for constitutional reform. Marie Antoinette had won her point. There must be no treating with what she called 'un amas de fous, de scélérats', 'a lot of idiots and rascals'.

On the next day, 20 June, while the King was hunting the stag at Le Butard, the rebels, finding the Salle de Menus Plaisirs shut, assembled in the Jeu de Paume, and the famous Oath of the Tennis Court followed where all but one deputy took an oath to uphold the National Assembly 'and to go on meeting wherever circumstances might dictate until the constitution of the kingdom and the regeneration of the state is firmly established'. From then on, as Mirabeau's secretary Dumont wrote later, the Third Estate was 'in league against the power of the throne'.

On 23 June 1789, the Ancien Régime, for the last time, met in all its magnificence at a royal session of the Estates. Surrounded by his wife and the princes, Louis XVI played the part of a blind despot. The decrees on taxes of 17 June had no force; the manorial tithes and rights would be maintained. 'If by a misfortune far from my mind,' the King concluded, 'you were to forsake me in such a great

RIGHT A bas-relief by Jules Dalou of the States General meeting on 23 June 1789, with the inscription: 'We are here by the will of the people and we shall not leave except at the point of bayonets.'

BELOW The opening of the States General at Versailles on 5 May 1789: an engraving by Helman after Monet, official Court painter to Louis.

133

The Oath of the Tennis
Court, 20 June 1789: one
of David's impressions of the
major events of the
Revolution.

135

enterprise, I should work alone for the good of the people and I should consider myself as being its only true representative.'

Outside some four thousand troops waited. They had been ordered to clear the hall when the session was over, but because of the mood of the crowd and their uncertain loyalty, they never even entered the building. When this was reported to Louis he merely exclaimed, 'They want to stay? Well, to hell with them, let them stay!' Secretly the King gave orders that six regiments should come to Versailles, while on 1 July, ten more regiments, mostly Swiss and German mercenaries, were drafted into the Paris area. Besenval, whose job was to 'control' Paris, was responsible for them all. The Assembly, alarmed, sent a deputation to the King on 9 July but he merely replied, 'Only the ill-disposed could mislead my people about the precautionary measures I am taking.' Already there was open unrest in Paris because of the price of bread which was in short supply. The city was crowded with hungry and unemployed people who had converged there in the vain hope of finding employment.

On 11 July Necker's dismissal was like the crack of a whip. All Paris knew of it the following day, when Camille Desmoulins, a young lawyer, journalist and agitator, leaped on to a bench in the gardens of the Palais Royal crying: 'I have just come from Versailles. Monsieur Necker is dismissed. This is the signal for a St Bartholomew's Day of the Patriots. This evening the Swiss and German battalions will cut our throats. We have but one resource – to take arms!' The answer was a general rising; military posts were seized, arsenals plundered, barricades erected. Versailles refused to recognize the gravity of the situation and unwisely Besenval decided to withdraw his forces and leave Paris to itself. On 14 July, twenty thousand men marched against the Bastille, reportedly impregnable but in fact quite unprepared for siege. Within a few hours it had been taken, de Launay, the governor, had been lynched by the crowd, and his head placed at the end of a long pike.

Later that evening the Duc de la Rochefoucauld-Liancourt galloped into Versailles from Paris, demanding to see the King, who was by now in bed and asleep. 'The Bastille has been taken by storm and the governor has been murdered. His head, at the end of a pike, is being paraded in triumph through the streets.' 'Are you bringing me news of a revolt?' asked the King. 'No, Sire, it is a Revolution.'

Louis XVI was to bring his diary to date: '13 July: nothing;

14 July: nothing.' Later, when the news from Paris had really sunk in, his first reaction was to abdicate. Marie Antoinette advised their immediate departure for the safety of Metz, the fortress town in Lorraine, not far from the German frontier. Instead, Louis went with his brothers to the Assembly and announced to the deputies the withdrawal of all troops from Paris. 'I am one with the Nation,' he declared to an enthusiastic audience. 'I entrust myself to you.'

The Place d'Armes outside the château was filled with an immense crowd who called for the King, Queen and new Dauphin to appear on the balcony. Marie Antoinette asked Madame Campan to find her son but to tell Madame de Polignac not to accompany the little prince. 'Ah, Madame,' said the Duchesse when she heard the Queen's order, 'what a blow this is!'

Madame Campan went down into the courtyard to mingle with the crowd just as the King and Queen with Madame Royale and the Dauphin appeared on the balcony. 'Ah,' said one woman, disappointed, 'the Duchesse is not with her.' 'No,' a man replied, 'but she is still at Versailles. She is like a mole. She is working underground, but we shall be able to dig her out.' Terrified, Madame Campan repeated what she had heard to Marie Antoinette who summoned the Duchesse. 'I fear the worst,' she told her. 'In the name of our friendship, leave me. You still have time to avoid the fury of my enemies. When they attack you they are more incensed against me than against you.' Madame de Polignac resisted in vain. When the King came in, Marie Antoinette begged him to order the couple to depart for their own safety. At midnight, Madame de Polignac was handed a letter from Marie Antoinette just as she and her husband were preparing to leave Versailles: 'Farewell, dearest of friends, the word is a dreadful one. Here is the order for the horses. Farewell, I have only the strength to embrace you.'

Not without difficulty, for at Sens they were almost recognized, they arrived at Basle. Soon they received a letter from Marie Antoinette: 'I can only venture to write a word, my dear love. . . . I cannot express all my regret at being separated from you; I hope you feel as I do. We are surrounded with nothing but grief, misfortune and unfortunates. . . . Everyone is fleeing and I am only too happy to think that all those I care for are far from me.' Fersen was at Valenciennes where he saw passing through the Comte d'Artois, the Prince de Condé, the Duc de Bourbon, the Duc d'Enghien, Vaudreuil and the Marquis de Polignac. Most of the

DÉPOT DES GARDES FRANÇOISES

Two engravings by Berthault after works by Prieur illustrating the violence of the Revolutionaries:
ABOVE French guards rush to the defence of their colonel, M. du Châtelet, and save him from the popular hysteria: 12 July 1789.
OPPOSITE Paris is guarded by the people on the night of 12/13 July 1789.

Queen's friends left Versailles: Coigny, Calonne, Lambesq, Luxembourg, the Marsans, Breteuil and even Abbé Vermond. She faced the storm alone.

One friend was not to leave her. Axel, Count Fersen was the only man to remain loyal when to appear in public as her friend brought no advantage, honour or respect. Seldom noticed, he kept in the background in case his help was needed. Saint-Priest, not entirely amiable, writes that Fersen used to go 'on horseback in the park, near the Trianon, three or four times a week; on her side the Queen did the same alone, and these meetings caused a great deal of public scandal in spite of the favourite's modesty and restraint, for he never showed anything outwardly and was the most discreet of all the Queen's friends'. Louis can have had few

138

illusions – if he did, they were well concealed. 'She found ways
and means of acquainting the King with the fact that she had a
liaison with the Comte de Fersen,' wrote Saint-Priest. But the
previous summer, while Fersen was in Sweden fighting for
Gustavus III against Russia, Louis XVI had received a packet of
letters one day when he was hunting. His equerries went away
as he sat down on the grass to read them. On their return they
found the King weeping bitterly and later, he revealed to Marie
Antoinette that the letters contained horrible accusations concerning herself and Fersen. 'They want to take from us the only
friend we can rely on,' she said, and proposed that they should
not receive the Swede when he returned. The King dissuaded
her and Fersen resumed his daily visits to the château.

Separated from most of her former friends, she came increasingly to seek her children's company. 'I have them with me as much as possible,' she wrote to Madame de Polignac. 'You have certainly heard of the appointment of Madame de Tourzel. It gave me much pain.' Madame de Tourzel, indeed, had been appointed governess to the two children of France, and it was for her benefit that, while the political storm was at its height, Marie Antoinette, shewing herself capable of shrewd judgment where her children were concerned, prepared the following report on 24 July:

My son is four years and four months old, less two days. . . . Like all strong healthy children he is very thoughtless, absent-minded and violent in his anger, but he is good-natured, gentle, and even affectionate when he is not carried away by his thoughtlessness. He has an extremely good opinion of himself which by good guidance might one day be turned to his advantage. He keeps his word faithfully once he has given it, but he is very indiscreet and easily repeats what he has heard and often, without meaning to lie, he adds things suggested by his imagination. This is his greatest fault and it must be firmly corrected. My son does not yet know how to read and he is a slow learner, being much too inattentive to think seriously about the task. He has no ideas of grandeur and I should wish that to continue. Our children learn all too soon the rank into which they have been born.

The events of the first month of the Revolution were also to bring Marie Antoinette closer to her husband. When the Assembly and the town of Paris, wishing simultaneously to humiliate Louis XVI and make him sanction the massacre of 14 July, asked him to visit his 'good town', he agreed to go despite Marie Antoinette's agonized pleadings. Like a man going to the scaffold, he left for Paris, having appointed Provence Lieutenant-General of the kingdom in the event of his not returning. Bailly, President of the National Assembly and new Mayor of Paris, welcomed him with the ambiguous words, 'Paris has achieved the reconquest of its King.' He was then made to pin to his hat the emblem of the Revolution: the tricolour cockade. The municipal revolution was thus recognized and Lafayette assumed command of the National Guard, an army of the people. Marie Antoinette, in the meantime, was convinced her husband would not return. 'A silence of death reigns over all the palace,' wrote Madame Campan. That evening, when the King came back to Versailles, she threw herself into his arms, weeping for joy.

August and September relentlessly brought further humiliations, further developments. The 4 August had seen the abolition of certain feudal rights. The nobles had to renounce *corvées* (statute labour) and tithes. The princes of the Church must forego their rents and revenues from the salt tax. Serfdom was abolished; the Press was declared free; the Rights of Man were proclaimed and the Third Estate became supreme. Freedom had been given to the written and spoken word, and freedom in its first exuberance was fierce and unmeasured. Journals outdid each other in the extravagance of their patriotism: Mirabeau founded one of his own, so did Desmoulins, Brissot, Loustalot and Marat. Rapidly the feudal system in France was breaking down and obviously its end was further hastened when the National Assembly declared that all men must be equal and without privilege. 'I will never consent to the spoliation of my clergy and my nobility,' said Louis concerning the Declaration of the Rights of Man of 3 August. 'I will not sanction such decrees.' But now the National Assembly, and Robespierre in particular, was questioning his power of veto. Eventually a compromise solution was reached whereby the King should have the right to suspend legislation for the life of two legislatures, but that was all. The King and Queen were now mocked with new nicknames: 'Monsieur and Madame Veto.'

While Versailles continued to hesitate and postpone, the cry of the revolutionary newspapers became more impatient. They summoned an end to this tedious bargaining between King and people: 'You have a hundred thousand, two hundred thousand fists; there are muskets and cannon in the arsenals; get them out ready for use; fetch the King and Queen from Versailles; take your destinies into your own hands!'

At Versailles, the royal family were somewhat isolated since the desertion of the French guards who had left for Paris during the night of 30-31 July with all their arms and baggage. A National Guard had been formed at Versailles, but this was hardly to be relied on. At the headquarters of the Revolution in the Palais Royal the Marquis de Huruge, one of the deserters from the Court, was ready at the slightest command to march on Versailles.

The Court now mustered their defences. One thousand men of the Flemish Regiment were posted to Versailles from Douai to protect the palace. On 1 October they were the guests of the Versailles garrison at a banquet in the Opera House of the palace. At first Marie Antoinette had not wished to attend the banquet, but after Louis returned from hunting, they went together to the Opera House and showed themselves in the royal box with their two children. The guests had dined well and when the royal family

Jean Sylvain Bailly, first Mayor of Paris: a contemporary portrait. He was not to survive the Revolution, but was guillotined a month after Marie Antoinette, in November 1793.

141

appeared, officers and men rose from their seats to toast the King and Queen. Marie Antoinette, moved by this enthusiastic reception, responded by walking twice round the banqueting table on the stage. She entrusted the Dauphin to an officer of the Swiss Guards who lifted the four-year-old boy on to the table. To everyone's delight, the child walked from one end of the horseshoe-shaped table to the other. As the King and Queen moved among their guests, an orchestra played Gretry's *O Richard, O Mon Roi* which, as it had strong royalist associations, was to prove unfortunate when the news reached Paris.

As was to be expected, the Paris pamphleteers transformed this happy evening into an orgy. The banquet provided the perfect occasion the agitators had been waiting for and Paris was in a ferment of indignation. The guests were said to have trampled drunkenly on the tricolour cockade. There was no bread in Paris; supplies had been held up for two days, making the already hungry desperate. According to the pamphleteers flour was being hoarded at Versailles where, to make matters worse, they were insulting the nation. In the streets there were cries of 'It is time to cut the Queen's throat.'

In the afternoon of 5 October, Marie Antoinette walked through the park to the Petit Trianon. Alone, she sat on a stone bench in the Grotto of Love to read a book. The sky darkened and it had already begun to rain when she saw a page running towards her. He brought her a letter from Monsieur de Saint-Priest. The women of Paris were marching on Versailles.

Early that morning, a young woman had broken into a guard-room in Paris and stolen a drum. Beating it through the streets, she was soon at the head of an ever-growing mob. With cunning psychology the instigators of the uprising had realized that while having no qualms about shooting down men, Louis could never give the order to fire upon women. Maillard, a tall, thin revolutionary, appeared from nowhere, took command of this disorderly, chaotic mass, organized it into an army and incited it to march on Versailles, ostensibly to demand bread though really in order to bring the King to Paris. Too late, Lafayette, commanding officer of the National Guard, appeared upon the scene; he was unable to prevent the march on Versailles. But Fersen had been quicker; at the first warnings of danger he had galloped off to Versailles, circumventing the army of women, the 'eight thousand Judiths' as Desmoulins emotionally called them.

That day, as usual, Louis had gone hunting. A messenger was

142

The march of the 'eight
thousand Judiths' on
Versailles, on 5 October
1789. The women, desperate
for food, hoped their plight
would touch the hearts of
the King and Queen.

sent to Meudon to fetch him back and at three in the afternoon
he galloped in through the main gate of the palace, scattering the
first handful of women who had already arrived from Paris. Gates
which had not been shut since the time of Louis XIV were closed
in their faces. The bodyguards, the Flanders Regiment and two
hundred men of the Versailles National Guard were drawn up in
battle array in the Place d'Armes. Not a single cartridge had been
distributed among them. That evening Louis's diary would record
that he had had a poor day's hunting, with the comment, 'interrupted by events'.

In the palace there was turmoil. Saint-Priest had suggested that
the main body of demonstrators should be prevented from reaching Versailles by stationing the battalion of the Flanders Regiment
on the bridge at Sèvres and another at St Cloud, while the Swiss
Guards were to hold the bridge at Neuilly. Then, from a position
of strength, the King could address them in person at Sèvres and,
if necessary, cavalry could then be used for their dispersal. Meanwhile Marie Antoinette and the royal family should go to Rambouillet where the Chasseurs of the Lorraine regiment were
stationed. The Queen, however, refused to be separated from her
husband, saying that if he was in danger she wished to be near
him. 'Sire,' warned Saint-Priest, 'if you let them take you to Paris
tomorrow, you will lose your crown.'

143

The hours drew on towards evening and it was now raining heavily. A confused murmur of voices was coming from the Avenue de Paris. The army of women was close at hand, their skirts drawn up over their heads as protection against the downpour. The vanguard of the Revolution was in Versailles. The opportunity for decisive action whether by resistance or by flight had been lost. Drenched to the skin, cold and hungry, their shoes filled with mud, the women marched up to the palace. It had taken them six hours to walk from Paris and by now their voices were hoarse with cold, wet and fatigue. Earlier, many of them had been to the National Assembly. 'The Chamber had been invaded by the people of Paris, and the arena was packed,' recorded an eye-witness. 'The galleries were full of women and men armed with scythes, sticks and pikes. The sitting had been suspended but someone came on behalf of the King to request the president to send a deputation to the château and to keep the Assembly in session.'

The group chosen to go to the palace consisted of five or six women with a number of deputies, accompanied by Mounier, President of the Assembly. With every conceivable honour this uncanny deputation was escorted into the halls of Versailles. Among the deputies was a large, genial man, Dr Guillotin, Professor of Anatomy at the University of Paris. Louis, courteous and friendly, received the ladies so well that Louison Chabry, a 'worker in sculpture' aged twenty, fainted with emotion and embarrassment on finding herself in Louis XVI's presence. The King made her smell spirits while in the background he heard cries from outside: 'We will bring back the Queen's head on the end of a pike.' 'Have you come to harm my wife?' Louis asked the women.

Just then came the news that Lafayette was marching on Versailles with thirty thousand men including the former French Guards. Saint-Priest immediately advised the entire royal family to remove themselves to Rambouillet or even Normandy. Marie Antoinette hurried into the children's apartments where she informed the sub-governesses: 'We are leaving in a quarter of an hour, get your things together and hurry!' But it was too late. What had been possible at four o'clock was no longer possible at eight. The crowd prevented the carriage from leaving the stables. Force would have been needed and the King refused to employ it. Marie Antoinette reluctantly was forced to give her counter-order: 'Go and tell those ladies that everything is changed. We are staying.'

144

On this night of 5-6 October Marie Antoinette remained astonishingly calm. 'Her countenance was noble and dignified', reports an observer, 'and her face was calm, and although she could have had no illusions as to what there was to fear, no one could perceive the least trace of anxiety. She reassured everyone, thought of everything and was far more preoccupied by all that was dear to her than with her own person.'

In tears, Louis had signed the Declaration of the Rights of Man. Still weeping, he ordered the bodyguards and the Flanders Regiment to leave their posts and to bivouac, the former in the Tapis Vert between the palace and the Grand Canal, and the latter in the courtyard of the Little Stables. Only the Versailles National Guard remained on parade. 'As wet as ducks', floundering and stumbling in the mud, Lafayette and his French Guards arrived half an hour after midnight. They were soaked to the skin, and too late for any effective action. Instead of stopping the demonstration before it left Paris, or at least keeping it under control, all Lafayette had been able to do was to form a shambling rearguard, following in the wake of the marching women. Dramatically, he now offered Louis his life: 'Sire, I bring you my head to save that of your Majesty.' He then asked Louis to let the former French Guards take over the posts they had deserted a month before and entrust them with guarding the château. For the second time that evening Louis abdicated his responsibility.

It was two o'clock before Louis XVI and Marie Antoinette went to bed in their separate apartments. They never dreamed that this was to be their last night at Versailles. Dismissing her servants, Marie Antoinette refused the protection of several gentlemen who wished to spend the night outside her door. All was quiet outside. It was still raining. Lafayette retired to the Hôtel de Noailles, a short distance from the chapel gate, went to bed and sank into a deep sleep. 'I had no anxiety,' he was to say later. 'The people had promised me they would remain calm.'

At six o'clock on Tuesday, 6 October, it had just begun to get light. Marie Antoinette was woken by a noise under her windows. With relief she learned that it was nothing more than the 'women of Paris who, not having found anywhere to sleep, were walking on the terrace'. She dozed off again, but suddenly, a few minutes later, a drum started beating and a shot was heard. The chapel gate was open. Armed with pikes, mattocks and muskets, the mob swarmed in, having failed to get in by the main gate, and, led by a guardsman of the Versailles militia who seemed to know the way, they started to climb the great staircase. The assault had a definite and preconceived aim: 'To the Queen's apartments!'

Already they were rushing up the steps leading towards the Queen's private suite. A few of the bodyguard tried to bar the entrance. Two of them were cut down and savagely murdered and within minutes the bleeding trophies were flaunted on pike points. But Miromarde, the third guardsman, had escaped and though wounded, was hastening up the stairs, shouting at the top of his voice: 'Save the Queen, they mean to kill her. I am alone facing two hundred tigers. My comrades have been driven out of their own hall.'

The cry did actually save her. He slammed the door and bravely faced the howling mob alone before he too died. A musket crushed his skull and killed him outright. Though the doors had been hastily barricaded, they were being broken down by crowbars and axes. Terrified, a lady-in-waiting burst into Marie Antoinette's room to warn her. She had time only to slip a petticoat over her nightdress and throw a shawl across her shoulders. Barefooted, her stockings in her hand, she fled along the corridor leading to the Oeil de Bœuf and through it, to the King's apartments. The door was barred. For five minutes the Queen and her ladies beat on it while the assassins were breaking into one room after another, stabbing her bed with their pikes and searching the cupboards. At last a servant inside heard their knocking and opened the door. Marie Antoinette could take refuge in her husband's suite. But the King was not there. Learning from a guard that she was in safety, he had gone to find the Dauphin. Marie Antoinette went in search of Madame Royale. Five minutes later they were all four reunited in Louis XVI's bedroom. They could hear the axes of the attackers on the door of the Oeil de Bœuf when suddenly the noise was stilled. The French guards had at last counter-attacked and managed to drive the mob down the staircase and out of the palace, though not from the courtyard.

Late again, Lafayette only now arrived on the scene with a strong body of grenadiers. Thenceforward he gained the contemptuous nickname: 'Général Morphée' ('General Morpheus'). He was in time only to save about thirty members of the bodyguard who had been taken prisoner by the mob and would have been murdered. Outside, the multitude, ten thousand in number, held the palace prisoner. No longer was there the faintest chance of escape. '*Le Roi à Paris! Le Roi à Paris!*' ('The King to Paris!') The chant became louder. Urged by Lafayette, Louis appeared on the

General Lafayette, contemptuously referred to by Fersen as 'the American': a portrait by Debucourt.

balcony of the state bedroom to be greeted only by cries of 'To Paris! To Paris!' Lafayette begged the crowd to retire, but no one moved.

All this was witnessed by Marie Antoinette who had not moved from the window enclosure. Madame Elisabeth, Louis's sister, was at her side, Madame Royale in front of her and, standing on a chair, the Dauphin watched bewildered. 'Mamma,' he kept saying, 'I'm hungry.' Suddenly a voice demanded: 'The Queen on the balcony.' Inside the room everyone saw her pale with anxiety as she stood undecided. Lafayette had advanced to her side: 'Madame, it is indeed necessary that you should do this in order to placate the

147

people.' 'I shall appear,' she answered, and holding her children by the hand, she came forward. 'No children! The Queen alone!' With a movement of her arms she pushed back the Dauphin and Madame Royale and appeared on the balcony, her hair dishevelled and dressed only in a flimsy wrapper.

She appeared, but she made no sign of obeisance. Defiant and alone she looked unflinchingly across the courtyard. So tense was the atmosphere that for a whole minute there was absolute silence. No one knew how it would end. Then she bowed her head and curtsied. An incredible cry went up: '*Vive la Reine!*' The crowd were cheering the woman whom, a few minutes before, they had attempted to murder. She withdrew to make way for the King and Lafayette who came out again on to the balcony. Over the noise of the crowd the King managed to make himself heard: 'My friends, I shall go to Paris with my wife and children. I trust all that is dear to me to the love of my good and faithful subjects.' Again Marie Antoinette appeared, this time with Lafayette. Gallantly he kissed her hand and there were more cries of '*Vive Lafayette! Vive la Reine!*' But she had been disillusioned too often to be deceived by this belated acclamation. As she re-entered the room there were tears in her eyes. To Madame Necker she said: 'They will compel us, the King and me, to go back with them to Paris while they carry in front the heads of our bodyguards on the tops of their pikes.'

At twenty-five minutes past one on the afternoon of 6 October the procession of the fallen monarchy and their Court left Versailles for ever. After the rain of the past twenty-four hours, it was now a calm autumn day. It took six hours to drive at a foot's pace from Versailles to Paris. In the royal carriage, Marie Antoinette leaned as far back as possible to avoid being seen. Her face bore 'the marks of violent grief'. From time to time the King covered his face with his handkerchief 'to hide the tears'.

As Marie Antoinette had feared, the heads of Monsieur de Hutes and Monsieur de Varicourt, the two bodyguards massacred in the invasion of the château, led the procession. Immediately in front of the royal coach went the cannon, with women astride the barrels. The chant was continuous: 'We are bringing back the Baker, the Baker's wife and the Baker's boy.' Behind them marched the disarmed guards, then, reportedly, two thousand Court carriages. In one of them rode Fersen, heavily disguised.

It was six hours before they pulled up at the gates of Paris. The Dauphin was weeping with hunger. By the flickering light of torches, Bailly, Mayor of Paris, welcomed the King and Queen:

'What a wonderful day, Sire, on which the Parisians hold your Majesty and his family in their city.' Exhausted by now, they were taken to the Hôtel de Ville where they were led to the window and between lighted torches were made to look out over the dense crowd assembled in the square outside. 'Long live the King, long live the Queen, long live the Dauphin, long live us all!' They were in a generous mood. For them, the Revolution was over. Fersen, in the meantime, had gone to wait for Marie Antoinette in the Tuileries, but Saint-Priest, fearing that it would endanger Marie Antoinette more, had asked him to withdraw.

It was nearly ten o'clock when the royal family drew up outside the Tuileries in their dusty carriages. It had been forsaken since the building of Versailles and unoccupied since Louis XIV's minority, over a century before. The rooms had been dismantled, the furniture removed, but by the light of borrowed candles a sort of camp was improvised for the royal family. 'How ugly everything is here, Mamma,' said the poor little Dauphin, used to the brilliance of Versailles. 'My son,' answered Marie Antoinette, 'Louis XIV used to live here and liked the place well enough. You must not be more exacting than he was.' The Dauphin's door would not shut and Madame de Tourzel, not daring to go to bed, watched all night by the child's little bed. Louis XVI seemed calm enough. 'Let us shake down as best we can,' he said. 'For myself, I am content.' Marie Antoinette was far from content. To Mercy she wrote: 'What has happened during the last four-and-twenty hours seems incredible. No description of it could be exaggerated and, indeed, whatever could be said would fall short of what we have seen and suffered.'

6
Flight of Midsummer 1789-91

A T SEVEN O'CLOCK THE NEXT MORNING the Queen was woken by the sound of women's voices and looking down from her window at the Tuileries, she saw an enormous crowd which repeatedly called her name. In terror the Dauphin flung himself into his mother's arms but she calmed his fears as she saw, to her own relief, that the crowd this time was a friendly one. The same mob of fish-wives who the day before had brought the royal carriage back from Versailles were now shouting for bits of ribbon and flowers off her hat, and when the Queen and Dauphin appeared they were wildly cheered. Marie Antoinette showed her astonishment in a letter she wrote that day to Mercy who, having escaped from Versailles, had fled to Chennevières where he had a property:

Do not be anxious, I am well. If one forgets where we are and how we came here we could be well content with the people's behaviour, particularly this morning. I talk to the people: soldiers, fish-wives all hold out their hands to me; I give them mine. . . . The people this morning demand that we stay. I said, speaking for the King who was beside me, that our remaining here depended on their behaviour; that we much wished to stay, but all hatred ought to cease and if any more blood were shed we would at once fly in terror. Those near me all swore that all violence was over.

But this time she had few illusions. After a highly successful visit which Louis had made to the Faubourg Saint-Antoine, Bailly was tactless enough to say to the Queen: 'Your Majesty must be overjoyed at the joy of the good citizens.' 'Yes,' Marie Antoinette replied, 'the citizens are good mannered when the Masters go to visit them, but they are extraordinarily savage when they in their turn visit the Masters!'

Little by little life organized itself at the Tuileries. The Queen and her children were at first cramped and uncomfortable. 'I have nowhere but my little high-perched room,' she wrote to Mercy. 'My daughter sleeps in the closet next to my room and my son in the great chamber.' It was here that Madame de Staël came to visit her in the first few days: 'She excused herself to us, saying: "You know I did not expect to come here." She looked beautiful and careworn and hers is a face that one would never forget.' Around her, the great empty rooms were being refurnished in a valiant attempt to restore a semblance of comfort and grandeur. On the first storey were the King's bedroom and reception rooms, a small bedroom for his sister, another for each of the children, and a small drawing-room. On the ground floor were Marie Antoinette's bedroom, reception-room and dressing-room, also a billiard-room

PREVIOUS PAGES The arrest of the royal family at Varennes during the night of 22 June 1791: the point of no return. The engraving is by Berthault.

Premier hommage des Habitans de Paris à la Famille Royale
le mercredi 7 Octobre 1789. lendemain de son heureuse arrivée dans cette Ville
    Famille Auguste et tendre avec transport cherie
    Lorsque nous vous voyons parmi nous réünie
    Que vous puissiez rester dans nos murs desormais
    C'est le vœu le plus doux de tous vos vrais Sujets

The royal family were given a surprisingly good reception when they appeared at the opera the day after their arrival in Paris. The verse expresses the hope that they will remain within its walls.

and dining-room. The two floors were connected not only by the original staircase but by a new flight of steps to whose door Marie Antoinette and Madame de Tourzel alone held the key. It had been built on this occasion as an added precaution.

At the end of October the faithful Princesse de Lamballe arrived to take up residence in the Pavillon de Flore and resumed her duties as 'Superintendent of Her Majesty's Household'. Though the number of Court officials had been drastically reduced, the traditions of Versailles still clung fast: there were the same valets,

OPPOSITE A contemporary
cartoon showing Louis
taking part in the Feast of
the Federation held on the
first anniversary of the
storming of the Bastille.
People of every rank wielded
spades in an immense
communal effort to finish the
uncompleted construction in
time for the celebrations.

the same liveries, even the same etiquette, though this was often
'overthrown by the presence of popular delegations and the repre-
sentatives of the Assembly'. Only the men of the Bodyguard had
been dismissed. Their place had been taken by Lafayette's National
Guards.

Surrounded by the ruins and relics of traditional splendour, the
Queen led a sad and monotonous existence. She rose early and
received Louis XVI and her children after breakfasting alone.
After Mass she would fill the long, empty hours by working at
large pieces of tapestry or embroidering a flowered jacket for the
Dauphin; sometimes she would read. After dining together at
one o'clock, the royal family would play billiards with the King.
A long lonely afternoon followed when Marie Antoinette would
receive the Princesse de Lamballe and the few remaining friends
not yet fled, who would help to calm the distress 'every day
aroused by a swarm of anonymous letters'. Supper was at eight-
thirty and at eleven they went to bed. When the weather was good,
Marie Antoinette would walk in the garden close to the palace,
and on other evenings might play cards with the King. Louis XVI
hunted no more; Marie Antoinette hardly left the palace. After
a few weeks of this existence Lafayette suggested they should
make occasional appearances in Paris to emphasize the fact that
they were in no sense prisoners of the Tuileries.

Prisoners they were, none the less. Surrounded by an army of
spies, their activities, their company, plans and above all their
correspondence were closely guarded. To get a moment's private
talk with her secretary Angeard, Marie Antoinette was forced to
receive him in her daughter's room and to make sure that no one
was listening at the door. 'I defy the whole world to find me out
in anything wrong,' she wrote to her sister Marie Christine. 'It
is an advantage to be so watched and followed, for all my words,
all my desires and all my actions are devoted to the King's happiness
in the first instance.' The discipline of extreme unhappiness and
misfortune had at last made the Queen come to her senses: 'My
role now is to keep altogether in the background and to try by
total inaction to make them completely oblivious of me. I only
want them to remember my courage. I must be without any kind
of definite influence either towards persons or affairs. They must
turn back to us when they learn truly how we think.'

For a time it seemed that appeals to reason might have some
weight. In February 1790, when Louis XVI paid a visit to the
National Assembly and spoke to the Deputies, he was rapturously

154

Hubert Robert's painting of the Feast of the Federation at the Champ de Mars. The triumphal arch was specially built and each company of the National Guard at Paris had a new flag designed.

applauded. The Queen and the royal children met him as he returned to the palace through the gardens of the Tuileries where many more of the Deputies had gathered. Marie Antoinette, in the garden, spoke to them of her respect for the liberty of the subject and her support of the King's views. 'I present to you my son,' she said. 'I will teach him to uphold those laws of which I trust he may one day be the stay and shield.' She was cheered with enthusiasm.

156

At the Feast of the Federation she was again received with good will. On the Champ de Mars in front of the Ecole Militaire the Queen attended this first celebration of 14 July wearing tricolour ribbons in her hair. In front of four hundred thousand people Talleyrand, Bishop of Autun, said Mass as the trumpets sounded in the background. Lafayette, followed by the Deputies, swore to remain faithful to the nation, and Louis himself took an oath to maintain the Constitution. Marie Antoinette was carried away by

157

this moving combination of patriotism and religion. Her sad face lit up and she lifted the little Dauphin in her arms to the cries of 'Long live the Queen', 'Long live the Dauphin.' 'If Louis had known how to take advantage of the Federation, we would have been lost,' Barnave was later to admit. That evening, on 'the first day of patriotism', people danced and embraced. For them, the Revolution was over.

The euphoria was soon to fade. The Jacobin revolt of the garrison at Nancy, which was followed by the harsh repression of General de Bouillé, set the Revolution on the move once more. Paris was quick to accuse the Queen of having encouraged the executions ordered by the General, and at the Opera the chorus from *Iphigénie*, 'Let us praise our Queen', was booed. Outside her window she would sometimes hear ringing out in the distance that menacing, repeated '*Ça ira, ça ira.*' There were even fears for her life when her entourage learned of plans to poison her. Marie Antoinette one day surprised her chief chambermaid in the act of substituting sugar in the bowl which stood on her washstand. She smiled sadly: 'You are putting yourself to most unnecessary trouble. They will not try to use poison against me. We have calumny now which is far better at killing people. That is the way they will destroy me.' Already there were prints which showed her clasping a grenadier of the National Guard in her arms, with the caption: 'Bravo, bravo, the Queen has hooked up with the country.' Even Lafayette was reported to be her lover, the man she so utterly despised.

Each day brought new troubles. Across the borders, Artois and Condé, pushed on by Calonne, were up in arms. Safe in their frontier retreats of Coblenz and Turin, they boasted of their intentions to march against this Revolution with foreign aid and deliver the King and his family. In vain the Queen addressed letter after letter to Joseph II imploring him to curb the enthusiasm of these unheroic and dangerous 'saviours'. Joseph died and Leopold who succeeded him shared none of his elder brother's affectionate feeling for his sister.

After a voluntary exile of five months Mercy had reappeared at Court. Fersen also had returned, and in spite of the constant surveillance, Marie Antoinette received him in her own apartments. At St Cloud where the royal family had 'obtained the right' to pass the summer, they were watched and followed everywhere by aides-de-camp of the 'American', as Fersen had christened Lafayette. One of them slept in Marie Antoinette's ante-chamber to 'take her orders' but even that, Lafayette was to hear from Saint-Priest,

does not prevent Fersen's visits. He has established himself at the village of Auteuil, staying with a friend of his, and so he goes to St Cloud under cover of the dark. A discharged soldier of the guard met him leaving the château at three in the morning. I thought it my duty to speak to the Queen. 'Do you not think,' I said to her, 'that the presence of the Comte de Fersen and his visits to the château may not be a source of danger?' She looked at me with that disdainful air which you know: 'Tell him yourself if you think it right to do so'

and the visits continued.

Fersen's main ambition was that the royal family should leave Paris and establish themselves for the time being at some frontier town where they would at least be safe. Such an exodus had also been advised by Mirabeau, the Deputy from Provence. For some time now this great hero of the Revolution had been seeking a *rapprochement* with the Court, promising 'loyalty, zeal, activity and energy' in return for financial encouragement. After much hesitation Marie Antoinette was finally persuaded by Mercy to give him an interview in a corner of the park at St Cloud. After three-quarters of an hour Mirabeau, who was conquered by the simplicity and 'proud dignity' of the Queen, asked permission to kiss her hand, and, as he turned to leave, whispered, 'Madame, the monarchy is saved.' To his nephew who was waiting for him near the gate of the park, he could not help remarking, 'She is truly great, very noble and very unhappy, but I shall save her.' He was later to add, 'The King has only one man with him, his wife.' The King was no help; he had been completely overtaken by events. 'When one discusses business with him,' said one of his Ministers, 'one feels as though one were talking of matters concerning the Emperor of China.'

Honoré, Vicomte de Mirabeau: an engraving by H. B. Hall. This volatile and licentious, but talented, aristocrat did all that was in his power to save the royal family, but was stunned by the lack of response: 'It is pitiable, one might think that the house where they sleep could be reduced to cinders and they would not even awaken.'

Mirabeau lost no time in writing to the Queen to lay before her his plan. The royal family should make an attempt to regain some of their lost popularity, and under the protection of a few faithful regiments should make for some neighbouring town such as Compiègne or Fontainebleau or, better still, Rouen. From there, it would be possible to treat with the National Assembly. 'Four enemies are advancing at the double: taxation, bankruptcy, the army, winter. We must take the bull by the horns, or rather we must prepare for coming events by guiding them. In two words, civil war is not certain but perhaps expedient.' 'How can Mirabeau bring himself to believe that we would ever provoke civil war?'

159

said the Queen, sending his letter on to Mercy. She refused to receive him a second time, but, when Mirabeau died a few months later, on 2 April 1791, she was quick to realize the implications. 'Our last chance has been taken from us,' she said to the King.

One by one the last of her friends were leaving for Italy, among them the Duchesse de Fitz-James and the Princesse de Chimay. Still the Princesse de Lamballe refused to desert her. Though she wrote reassuringly to the fugitives, Marie Antoinette in a letter to the Duchesse de Fitz-James, showed her growing distress: 'I can give you no more news of this country. Each day, each hour, makes a lie of what one has just heard. There is nothing constant, nothing consecutive, nothing real except our profound unhappiness.' Her children, 'Mousseline' and 'Chou d'Amour' as she called them, were now her main joy. 'They are nearly always with me and are my consolation,' she wrote to Madame de Polignac, their former governess. 'If I could be happy I should be so by reason of these two little creatures. Chou d'Amour is charming and I love him dearly. He loves me very much too, in his way. . . . He is well, grows strong and no longer becomes angry. He goes for a walk every day which does him much good.'

Fersen also brought her comfort. Of the four people who shared the confidence of the King and Queen, Fersen alone was in Paris. General Bouillé was in command at Metz, Breteuil and Mercy had taken refuge in Brussels. In the spring of 1790 he was able to see Marie Antoinette 'easily and in her own apartments and that is some consolation for the knowledge of all the evils she has to endure . . . poor woman, she is like an angel in her behaviour, courage and feeling; never could one love another like her'. A few days later he was to write to his sister Sophie: 'She is extremely unhappy but very brave. I try to console her as best I can. I owe her that; she has been so perfect to me.' His dearest wish was to help the royal family escape from Paris while time still allowed. Marie Antoinette's attempts to convince her unwilling husband of this necessity were made all the more difficult by the near failure of Mesdames Adelaide and Victoire's secret escape from Paris on 19 February 1791.

It was hardly an encouraging sign, and Louis was soon to abandon his feelings of loyalty towards the Revolution. Early in 1791 he had been forced to sign the decree concerning the civil constitution of the clergy. 'I would rather be King of Metz', he had said to Fersen, 'than remain King of France in such conditions.' Only Talleyrand and Gobel and half the *curés* of France took the

160

oath to the constitution, but the others ran the risk of being labelled 'non-jurors' in their defiance of the National Assembly. On 10 March the Pope condemned the civil constitution of the clergy and, as Easter drew nearer, the question of the King's duties became crucial. The unexpected death of Mirabeau on 2 April had robbed the King of his main hope and he decided therefore on a public trial of strength. On Palm Sunday Louis heard Mass said by Cardinal de Montmorency but refrained from receiving communion though he was a non-juring priest. On his return from the chapel, the grenadiers of the National Guard refused to line the route, but Louis next announced his intention of going to St Cloud for Easter. There was an outcry in the Jacobin Press headed by Marat in *L'Ami du Peuple*, who immediately assumed he was leaving Paris to fulfil his Easter duties 'unconstitutionally'. On 18 April, the following

An effigy of the Pope is burned outside the Palais Royal on 6 April 1791: an engraving by Berthault after Prieur. Pope Pius VI had condemned the civil constitution of the clergy, which imposed secular reforms on the organization of the Church in France.

161

day, the carriages had hardly left the courtyard of the Tuileries when they were surrounded by a howling mob. Lafayette and Bailly, with no success, ordered the National Guard to clear a passage, and for two hours the royal family remained thus besieged, with insults freely hurled through the windows. As they finally reascended the steps of the Tuileries, the Queen was heard to remark sharply to her husband, 'You must admit now that we are no longer free.'

In face of these repeated humiliations Louis was driven to accept flight as the only recourse. Marie Antoinette announced this decision to Mercy in the following terms: 'Our position is awful and only those close at hand can have any idea of it. . . . Do not think that I exaggerate our dangers. You know that the means I have relied on and urged as far as I could have been gentleness and a change in public opinion; but today everything is changed. . . . We must perish or take some action, that is the only alternative left.' From his headquarters at Metz, the Marquis de Bouillé was to send two detachments to meet the fugitives who would then make their way to Montmédy, a strong frontier town where Louis XVI could assemble troops 'and those of his subjects who were still faithful to him and could win back the rest of his people led astray by seditious leaders'. They planned to avoid Reims where the King was afraid of being recognized, and go by Châlons, Sainte-Menehould, Varennes, Dun and Stenay.

It was Fersen who had undertaken to arrange the departure. Already, by the end of December, he had ordered, at the Queen's request, a large berlin, painted outside in green and yellow and upholstered in white Utrecht velvet, a conspicuous vehicle for such a secret journey. For two months before the departure Fersen passed daily in and out of the Tuileries by an unguarded door to keep Marie Antoinette informed of the plans and bring her Bouillé's ciphered despatches. Passports were acquired in the name of a Russian noblewoman, Baronne de Korff, *en route* for Frankfurt. She was to be impersonated by Madame de Tourzel who was also to be the mother of the two children. The Queen became the governess with the name of Madame Fochet and Louis was to be Durand, the Baronne's steward. In a lighter, smaller carriage were to travel two ladies-in-waiting as Madame de Korff's maids. With Madame Elisabeth and three bodyguards disguised as couriers, the number was brought to eleven. Had Marie Antoinette consented to a more humble escape the project might well have been successful. The Comte and Comtesse de Provence, who fled the same night,

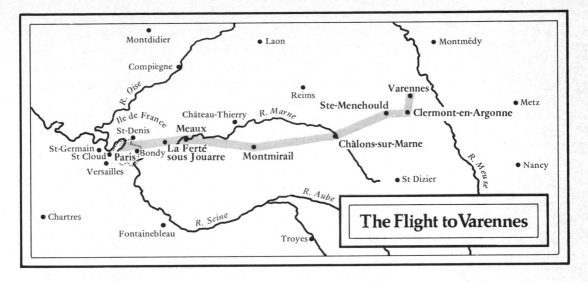

The Flight to Varennes

travelled light and fast and were in Brussels before the royal family had even reached Châlons-sur-Marne. Marie Antoinette's concern for her own comforts was to prove disastrous. The brightly painted berlin could hardly help but attract attention, especially since it had to be made large enough to take the entire family, several large trunks full of new clothes for the arrival at Montmédy and a magnificent travelling-case ordered two months before from the jewellers. Léonard, her hairdresser, was ordered to make his own way to the frontier at the same time. At each stage they would have to order six draught-horses for the berlin, three horses for the cabriolet carrying the two ladies-in-waiting Marie Antoinette considered essential, and two post-horses for the couriers. A conspicuous number.

Their main hazard was to leave the Tuileries without being seen. Every exit was heavily guarded by a division of six hundred men under arms. In the courtyards, in the gardens, along the terrace, sentries were permanently on the watch, while within the difficulties were even greater. The corridors that led to the apartments of the King and Queen were guarded, so was the small service corridor under the roof and the back stairs that led to it. Fersen promised to 'be responsible for this delicate operation' and, to the outside eye, the evening of 20 June 1791 seemed as any other. Earlier that day Marie Antoinette, Madame Elisabeth and the children had walked in the Tivoli garden and, on their return, had ordered a carriage for the following day. After supper that evening the King, Madame Elisabeth and the Comte and Comtesse

163

de Provence were with Marie Antoinette in her reception-room on the ground floor of the palace. At ten o'clock she rose calmly and went to her daughter's room. There she told the undergoverness to dress Madame Royale, explaining the situation to her and informing her that she too was to make the journey with Madame de Neuville, the Dauphin's waiting-woman. Next she went to the Dauphin's room where she found him already awake. 'We are going to a place of battle where there will be many soldiers,' she told her son. The child, delighted, asked for his boots and sword, but instead of his French guard's uniform he was brought a girl's dress. He soon recovered from his disappointment, and when his sister asked him later 'what he thought they were going to do', he replied happily, 'We are going to act a play, for we are in disguise.'

First to leave the palace were Madame Royale, the Dauphin and Madame de Tourzel. With them went Marie Antoinette and one of the bodyguard. Reaching the antechamber which led on to the Cour des Princes by an unguarded glass door, the Queen looked first into the courtyard. A silhouette could be seen behind the window lit by the carriage lamps and torches. It was Fersen, dressed in his coachman's great-coat. Coming forward, he took the Dauphin's hand and led Madame de Tourzel and Madame Royale to a waiting fiacre. Taking the reins in his hands, he quietly drove out of the courtyard. The vehicle, after making a detour by the quays at the Place Louis XV, would wait in the Rue de l'Echelle at the corner of the Place du Petit-Carrousel. Marie Antoinette returned unnoticed to the drawing-room where the Comte de Provence was ready to leave. 'We embraced tenderly and separated,' he said later.

In her bedroom she calmly gave orders for her walk the next day as her women undressed her and put her to bed as usual. There was not a hint of suspicion. As soon as her ladies had left the room, Marie Antoinette got out of bed, put on a grey dress, a black mantle and a large hat with a violet veil thick enough to make her face unrecognizable. With Monsieur de Malden, one of the disguised bodyguards, she reached the Place du Petit Carrousel in safety. At that moment came the sudden light of torches as Lafayette's carriage rode past. Satisfied that all was quiet, he was returning from his night rounds of inspecting the Tuileries. Swiftly the Queen drew back into a shadowed doorway, as the carriage passed within touching distance of her. Further on she found the fiacre and rejoined Fersen and her children. Madame Elisabeth had already reached the meeting-place, but now they all waited for the King. His *coucher*, which Lafayette had attended, had been far longer than usual and it was midnight before they were all assembled and Fersen could mount the box to drive the carriage towards the St Martin barrier.

They were already two hours behind schedule, and there was a further delay as they looked for the berlin which they found at last, hidden down a sidestreet with its lamps veiled. Quickly the royal family climbed in and by two o'clock Fersen was whipping the horses towards Bondy, which they reached in less than an hour. Here Fersen was to leave the party. The King, for some reason, had been opposed to the idea of his going further. '*Il n'a pas voulu*' ('He did not wish it'), remarked Fersen. Midday should see them passing through Châlons-sur-Marne, and by about four o'clock they should meet the first of the troops under Choiseul, nephew of Louis XV's minister, at Pont-de-Somme-Vesle. The early dawn of midsummer was already breaking when Fersen called out in a loud voice to deceive the uninitiated postillions: '*Adieu Madame de Korff*' and galloped off on the road to Brussels from whence he would rejoin the fugitives.

Inside the berlin the royal party began to relax. The King regained some of his old confidence. 'Believe me,' he said, 'when I have my backside on a saddle I shall be very different from what you have seen up to now.' Hungrily, they 'attacked the canteen' prepared by Fersen: *bœuf à la mode* and cold veal. They ate 'without plates or forks like hunters or economical travellers'. Marie Antoinette, from her window, offered the bodyguards something to eat and drink as she said jokingly to Malden, 'Perhaps at this moment Monsieur de Lafayette's head is no longer on his shoulders.'

In Paris, Lafayette had just been awoken with the news of the King's escape. As he threw on his uniform, he could hear an approaching 'murmur like the roar of a wave driven by the storm'. All Paris 'intoxicated by being for the first time without a master' was filling the streets. He ordered men of the National Guard to fan out in all directions, scouring the most likely roads for the King and his family. At Clermont-en-Argonne, the last post before Varennes, the population was uneasy at the presence of 180 dragoons and from Châlons-sur-Marne to the frontier, villagers all along the route had their doubts about these troops 'waiting to escort treasure'. At Ste-Menehould the National Guard was issued with new muskets and at the hamlet of Pont-de-Somme-Vesle curiosity would soon be aroused by the arrival of forty

165

A page from Louis's diary, recording the events of the flight to Varennes, punctuated as always by the ubiquitous 'Rien'.

hussars from Varennes. Choiseul, their commanding officer, arrived simultaneously from Paris. With him was Léonard, the Queen's hairdresser.

At the small relay stations on the road to Châlons the King would get out of the berlin 'to gossip with individuals of the people who came to see the travellers'. Moustier was anxious at this rashness but Louis was confident: 'Don't bother. I do not think this precaution necessary. I feel my journey is safe from all accidents.' Unknown to them all, a horseman in full pursuit had already crossed the St Martin barrier. Commissary Bayon, by chance, had taken the Metz road, not knowing he was galloping in the right direction. The fugitives were a good ten hours in front of him, but their progress was becoming slower as their confidence increased.

At the bottom of the long steep hill that led into Étoges, Marie Antoinette got out of the carriage 'in order to refresh herself'. It was a stifling hot day. Taking her husband's arm, they both followed the berlin which slowed down to walking pace, while Madame Royale and her brother started chasing butterflies by the roadside.

In Paris the Jacobin club had just voted a resolution: 'Louis has abdicated from the monarchy; henceforth Louis is nothing to us. We are now free and without a King.' A second horseman was now on the way. Romeuf, Lafayette's aide-de-camp, had picked up the trail at Bondy and though he carried a decree of the Assembly ordering the King's arrest, a Royalist at heart, he hoped to overtake Bayon and throw him off the scent.

At Pont-de-Somme-Vesle Choiseul and his forty hussars had been expecting the berlin to arrive at one o'clock. It was now almost four. Their anxiety increased as peasants from the surrounding district began to form a menacing crowd around the relay station. They had failed to pay their taxes and imagined that these hussars had come to take punitive action. The carriage, at that moment, rapidly driven, was entering the suburbs of Châlons. It was to change horses at the other end of the town, and in spite of the crowd assembled at the post-house, everything went off without incident. Bayon, his horse foaming at the mouth, changed mounts at La Ferté. Romeuf had just left Meaux, having covered eleven leagues in two and a half hours.

Choiseul, taking as his excuse the King's delay and the excitement around the relay station, decided to abandon his post of 'advance sentry'. He sent Léonard ahead to warn the detachments at Ste Menehould and Clermont 'that there was no sign of the treasure passing today'. Less than half-an-hour later the berlin rumbled into Pont-de-Somme-Vesle, shaken to find that the escort had already left. Behind them Bayon was gaining ground. At Chaintrix he learned from the post-master that the fugitives were only three hours ahead of him. But he was exhausted. He had ridden thirty-five leagues in six hours and changed horses ten times. Someone offered to go on in front and the officer scribbled an order: 'On behalf of the National Assembly all good citizens are ordered to stop the berlin with six horses in which the King and Queen are suspected of travelling.'

At Ste Menehould Captain Dandoins, after Léonard had gone through, dismissed his dragoons who then wandered through the streets 'in police caps and stable dress'. Soon after seven o'clock the berlin rolled into the main street. Marie Antoinette, recognized by a few of the troops, gravely bowed her head to their salute, thereby admitting her identity. The carriages stopped at the post-house. Drouet, the post-master, had that moment come in from the fields and was standing by the carriage when someone came up to him and handed over *assignats* as payment for the relay of the horses. One for fifty francs had the King's head on it. Drouet looked at the note and then at the Baronne de Korff's 'steward'. He recognized the King.

The berlin rolled slowly over the Argonne fields. Behind them at Ste Menehould the rumour ran from horse to horse 'that the King and Queen have just passed'. The tocsin sounded, the dragoons were dismissed, and when Bayon's messenger arrived, Drouet and his friend Guillaume leaped into the saddle and galloped down the road taken an hour before by the berlin. It was now half-past nine. At Châlons, Romeuf had just caught up with Bayon and, on arriving at the Hôtel de Ville, he announced that he would go quickly on his way. Bayon at that moment appeared. He had intended to go to bed but now 'begged for the honour' of accompanying Lafayette's aide-de-camp. Reluctantly Romeuf agreed, and they galloped off together.

The royal coach had just changed horses at Clermont and soon afterwards had left the main Metz road to take the turning on the left to Varennes. After Varennes was Stenay, Montmédy and safety. Another forty miles and it would all be over. Léonard, tragically misinformed, was still tearing along ahead of them saying they were not coming. Varennes did not have a post-house, but General Bouillé's son was waiting there with a fresh team stabled in one of the two hotels. All of a sudden, Léonard came rushing down the hill. He stopped the soldiers and, without even getting out of the carriage, he pushed his head through the window and said: 'I am Léonard. I know all! The King has left Paris but there is no sign of him having continued his journey.' Then he was on his way again towards Stenay and freedom.

Convinced that the detachments of Ste Menehould and Clermont were galloping behind, the berlin, with its lamps lit, rolled along the road towards Varennes. Two leagues back were Drouet and Guillaume galloping at full speed. Thanks to a short cut they had avoided the bend at Clermont. Drouet had met his postillions on their return journey and learned that the berlin had left the main road. In the Argonne forest, Choiseul and his exhausted horsemen, having tried a short cut from Pont-de-Somme-Vesle to Varennes,

168

were now wandering hopelessly about. They had lost the path.

At half-past ten the berlin reached the first houses of the upper town of Varennes. Ahead of them the street was deserted. Because of Léonard, Bouillé and his fellow officers Röhrig and Raigencourt had gone to their billets for the night. The carriage came to a halt as one of the party went in search of the missing horses and the escort of the dragoons. No one noticed two horsemen who galloped past the carriage and descended into the lower town. A little further on, Drouet and Guillaume dismounted outside the Bras d'Or inn. Ten minutes later the trap was ready. A cart full of furniture barred the little bridge over the Aire. The *procureur* of the district, the grocer Sauce, had been woken and with several National Guards took up his position at the end of a vaulted passage. Standing against the walls, they waited for the berlin, which could take no other road.

A few moments later, the Queen and her family were once more prisoners of the Revolution. All Varennes had been awoken and the tocsin rang urgently. Bouillé's son and Captain de Raigencourt were the last to hear of the King's arrest. Leaping to their saddles, they disappeared in the direction of Montmédy to warn General de Bouillé who was at Stenay with the Royal German Regiment. Crowds were gathering in front of the grocery run by Monsieur Sauce, a plain wooden house where the royal family had been taken. That moment, Choiseul and his forty horsemen at last rode into Varennes, but even now Louis refused to allow them to use force at a time when they might have been able to snatch the royal family from the hands of the municipality. The arrival of General de Bouillé was now their only hope and the hours passed as, tense and full of hope, the prisoners sat in cane chairs waiting for the rescue that would surely come.

Suddenly, at five in the morning, the door burst open as Bayon and Romeuf entered the little room. Romeuf had tears in his eyes as he held out the decree from the National Assembly: 'Order to all functionaries to arrest all the members of the royal family.' 'What, Monsieur, you? I should not have expected it from you,' cried Marie Antoinette who had seen the aide-de-camp every day at the Tuileries. 'There is no longer a King of France,' said Louis dully, as he dropped the piece of paper on to the bed where the children were asleep. At this Marie Antoinette lost her self-control. 'I will not have it contaminating my children,' she cried, as she snatched the decree and flung it violently to the ground.

Outside, ten thousand people were howling under the windows:

'To Paris! To Paris!' In vain Marie Antoinette and the King tried one delaying tactic after another. They asked that the children should be allowed to sleep a little longer. They requested food, and Madame de Neuville even simulated an epileptic fit. All their efforts were seen through and at last Louis XVI was forced to give orders to harness the carriage. At half-past seven on the morning of 22 June the royal family climbed once more into the berlin. It was going to be another long hot summer day. Quarter of an hour later, from the other side of the river, General de Bouillé and the Royal German Regiment could just see the great coach trundling down the road towards Clermont and Paris with four thousand men as guard. Thinking the river too deep to ford, he ordered the retreat to be sounded. Had he but known, the Clermont road crossed the Aire only half a mile further on, and if his troops had galloped across the fields, they could have cut off the berlin and taken the royal family in safety to Montmédy only thirty miles away.

The journey to Varennes had taken twenty-four hours. It took them four days to return. The intense heat and unparalleled demonstrations of hatred made the journey back a living nightmare. At Châlons, where the triumphal arch erected for her joyful entry as Dauphine now served as a mocking reminder, Marie Antoinette was met by a crowd of nearly five thousand who, with hatred in their eyes, brandished the remains of the Comte de Dampierre. He had just been massacred for daring to salute the Queen. Marie Antoinette, 'in a state of prostration hardly to be conceived', was forced to watch the appalling spectacle. The berlin, out of Châlons, was to leave its original route and travel towards Épernay and Dormans. After Château-Thierry it would rejoin the old route at La Ferté-sous-Jouarre. Not far short of Dormans the huge procession came to a halt. Three Deputies, Latour-Mauborg, Barnave and Pétion, were waiting to escort Louis along the last stage of the journey back to Paris.

While Latour-Mauborg travelled with the waiting-women, Barnave and Pétion squeezed into the berlin as best they could. Barnave, not as deeply committed to the Revolution as Pétion, was embarrassed at first to find himself seated next to Marie Antoinette, whom he had denounced so often in the Assembly. But as the journey progressed, he unconsciously found himself being won over by this proud woman with sad eyes. Not expecting the royal family's 'air of simplicity', he was taken aback by 'the easy ways and family good humour' of the travellers. The Dauphin, fidgeting, came to sit on his lap and, playing with the brass buttons on the

The return of the royal family to Paris on 25 June 1791. The crowds maintained a hostile silence and not one raised his hat: they had thrown off the yoke of servitude for good. A contemporary print.

Deputy's uniform, he slowly spelled out the inscription: '*Vivre Libre ou Mourir*' ('To live freely or to die'). Barnave, in spite of his political convictions, was deeply moved. His eyes filled with tears and he was soon to devote himself to Marie Antoinette's interests.

They had now reached the last stage of their journey. In the forest of Bondy on the outskirts of Paris, 'a crowd of madmen' came out of the wood and threw themselves on the National Guards. 'In vain were they driven back, they slipped under the horses and between the wheels' in their attack on the carriage. Marie Antoinette received the worst insults. Harridans uttered dreadful cries: 'The bitch, the slut, the whore.' As they entered Paris, she appeared to be suffering deeply. The Dauphin 'stood at the window looking at the people' while Louis seemed altogether dazed, 'the look of a drunken man', reported a witness. The three bodyguards were chained together on the seat; one of them was weeping. As they entered the Tuileries, Lafayette, who 'commanded the whole crowd with the dignity of a hero', came forward with 'affection and respect', as he himself asserted. His face was radiant. Marie Antoinette, who could not conceal her 'irritation', went straight to her rooms. Her hair, ash-blonde five days before, was now said to be quite white, 'like that of a woman of seventy'.

Two days before, Fersen had learned of the catastrophe from Bouillé himself. Marie Antoinette wrote to console him when she returned to the Tuileries: 'I exist. . . . How anxious I have been about you and how I pity you. . . . I shall not be able to write to you again.'

171

7
Borrowed
Time
1791-2

THE PALACE OF THE TUILERIES now wore every appearance of the prison it had become. Sentries were posted everywhere, even on the roofs of the château, while officers took it in turns to sleep behind a screen in the Queen's bedroom. Two or three times a night they came in to check she was in her bed. Lafayette went so far as to examine the chimney in case Marie Antoinette decided to escape from the roof, and rare visits from outside were so heavily scrutinized that it became almost impossible to enter. Louis now sank into a deeper state of apathy than ever before and occupied himself in the trivial satisfaction of statistics. 'From 1775 to 1791', he wrote in his private journal, 'I went out 2,636 times.' Marie Antoinette accepted her fate with less equanimity. When on 26 June the deputies arrived to ask questions about the Varennes episode, she silently and with icy dignity waved them to armchairs while she sat on a low stool in front of them.

Faced with her husband's incapacity, Marie Antoinette boldly, but rashly, decided to take over the responsibilities of government herself. To some extent events were to play into her hands. The flight to Varennes had precipitated a new phase in the history of the Revolution with the birth of the Republican party. On 15 July the Cordeliers joined with the Jacobins in demanding the abolition of the monarchy. But many of the latter felt this measure to be too extreme and 256 of the more right-wing deputies broke away to form the Feuillants, refusing to take any further part in the work of the Assembly. This left the Constitutionals, headed by Barnave, facing the left-wing Jacobins. The centre group was quick to realize that in order to protect the whole edifice built by the Constituent Assembly, it would have to stand with the threatened King. At the beginning of July, through the intermediary of General de Jarjayes, husband of one of her waiting-women, Marie Antoinette got into touch with Barnave. 'Tell him', she wrote, 'that I was struck with his personality which I recognized during those two days we spent together, and that I should very much like to know from him what there is for us to do in our present position.'

Barnave read the note several times 'with delight'. Moved by the good intentions displayed by Marie Antoinette and his dread of Republicanism, he assumed the role of mediator. The Assembly was stirred by his speech to 'maintain' the King but he was 'suspended' until he should be presented with the new constitution on which the Assembly was working. Barnave advised the Queen to let her 'present intentions' be publicly known. She could

174

L'HOMME
DE LA COUR.
1789

L'HOMME
DU PEUPLE.
1791.

prove these by convincing her brother Leopold and the *émigrés* that the King and Queen wished to become constitutional monarchs. Provence and Artois must return to the kingdom, and the Emperor of Austria must recognize the future constitution. He put it strongly to her that she could 'neither adopt other ideas nor leave this path without being ruined'. A few days later, when the National Assembly threatened to seize the *émigrés'* property if they did not return, Marie Antoinette said sharply to Barnave that it 'seemed impossible to her that people who had voluntarily left their country two years before should take part in negotiations when a large part of their fortune had been taken from them'. She graciously added that although she had no influence with her brother Leopold II, she 'did not refuse to write to him'. This hint of arrogance prompted Barnave to warn her again that the Triumvirs, the centre group, would turn against her if she did not co-operate.

A serious incident on Sunday, 17 July, showed the King and Queen the importance of co-operation. The extreme left had summoned their supporters, six thousand strong, to the altar in the Champ de Mars to sign a Republican petition. Two *voyeurs* who had hidden under the altar platform in order to peep up the ladies' skirts were spotted and taken for spies. Both were brutally massacred and their heads were paraded through the city on pikes. Martial law was declared, troops invaded the Champ de Mars and fifty people were killed as a result of a firing incident. A wedge was now driven between the constitutional and the advanced deputies. The latter, headed by Danton, Desmoulins and Santerre, went into temporary hiding. Marie Antoinette now seemed to show more goodwill towards the Triumvirs and was decidedly more accommodating. She asked both for an interview with them and for the draft of a letter she could copy and send to the Emperor.

The goodwill, unfortunately, was almost entirely on the part of the Triumvirs. Marie Antoinette was engaged in a sinister double game. She had not the slightest intention of following these 'exaggerated ideas' and had entered into the correspondence only in order to 'temporize'. She wrote to Mercy on 29 July asking him to warn Leopold to pay no attention to the letter dictated by the Triumvirs. It was necessary, she explained, that 'at least for some time to come' the duped leaders should think she was 'of their opinion' until the Allies could intervene and save her.

Her anxieties were all the more increased by hearing no news of Axel Fersen since her return. At a loss, she wrote to Esterhazy:

Revolutionary fashion, 1791: dress became more informal; the wide *paniers* which held out the skirts were discarded and printed muslins replaced brocades and silks.

'If you write to him tell him that many miles and many countries can never separate hearts. I feel this truth more strongly every day.' She sent two rings, which 'are sold everywhere here', engraved outside with three *fleurs-de-lis* and inscribed on the inside: '*Lâche qui les abandonne*', 'Faint-heart, he who forsakes her'. 'The one wrapped in paper is for him. Ask him to wear it for me. I wore it for two days before packing it. Tell him it comes from me. I do not know where he is. It is torture to have no news and not even to know where the people one loves are living.' She was to remain without news of him until the end of September. Fersen, at that time, was in Vienna trying with equal difficulty to interest Leopold II in his sister's fate and to prevent the *émigrés* from doing harm. Marie Antoinette, too, was full of dread for this noisy band of agitators. 'You know yourself', she wrote to Mercy, 'the *émigrés*' evil talk and evil intentions. After abandoning us, the cowards want to insist that we alone should expose ourselves and that we alone should serve their interests.' Fersen, writing from Brussels, described the Comte d'Artois as 'positively radiant' when he learned of the King's arrest. Their unheroic behaviour had even more serious implications, as during August the Assembly were occupied in drafting the future Constitution. For Marie Antoinette, the Constitution could be nothing more than a restriction of the Crown's authority, but until the Allies came to her assistance, she could only play for time.

177

The Constitution, accepted by the Assembly only through the
unceasing efforts of Barnave and his friends, left at least the appearance of authority to Louis. He had the right to veto decrees if he
so desired and the right to nominate ministers, ambassadors and
army chiefs; but the National Assembly alone would have the
right to declare war. To the advanced deputies it represented 'a
step backwards' and led to Barnave's being described by Robespierre and Pétion as 'an infamous cheat sold to the Austrian party'.
To Marie Antoinette, however, it seemed 'a tissue of insolence and
impractical absurdities'. She never stopped to think that this
'absurdity' might be the only means of saving the monarchy. To
Barnave she gave her apparent approval, on 31 August: 'Certainly
there are advantages to be gained from the constitution both for
the King and for the monarchy. . . . My trust in the courage, firmness and intelligence of those who wish for what is good, reassures
me.' But three days before, she had written to Mercy: 'It is not
possible to go on existing like this. All we have to do is to hood-
wink them and make them trust us so as better to defeat them
afterwards.' On 14 September Louis went to the Manège and
before the National Assembly, who denied him even the honour
of standing while he delivered his speech, he took the oath to the
Constitution and was formally reinstated as King. On his return
to the Tuileries he sank into an armchair and burst into tears. 'And
you were a witness to this humiliation!' he said to Marie
Antoinette. 'You came to France to see that!'

Convinced yet again that the Revolution was over, the deputies
dispersed to their provinces. Barnave and his friends, though
triumphant with their success, were uneasy none the less at 'the
languor and apathy' of Louis XVI and what they called 'the
Queen's uncertain and irresolute conduct'. Marie Antoinette
hastened to confirm her good intentions by writing to Barnave
that she was 'completely frank and I always shall be in everything,
for such is my character. I have always sacrificed my prejudices.'
Only the day before, she had written to Fersen: 'Set your mind at
rest, I am not going over to the madmen, and if I have relations
with some of them it is merely to make use of them. They revolt
me too much for me ever to go over to their side.' Marie Antoinette
was playing a dangerous double game, and it was one that she
could never fully control. Far worse was the fact that she was
coldly deceiving loyal, honest and sincere people, who, because
they believed in her and tried to save her, would one day lose
their lives. At the end of September the old National Assembly

178

DÉCRET

DE L'ASSEMBLÉE NATIONALE.

Du *trois Septembre* 1791.

La Constitution
française.

Déclaration des
droits de l'homme et du Citoyen.

Les Représentans du Peuple Français,
constitués en Assemblée Nationale, considérant
que l'ignorance, l'oubli ou le mépris des droits de
l'homme sont les seules causes des malheurs publics
et de la corruption des Gouvernemens, ont résolu
d'exposer, dans une Déclaration solemnelle, les droits
naturels, inaliénables et sacrés de l'homme, afin
que cette Déclaration, constamment présente à tous les
Membres du Corps social, leur rappelle sans
cesse leurs droits et leurs devoirs ; afin que les
actes du pouvoir Législatif et ceux du pouvoir

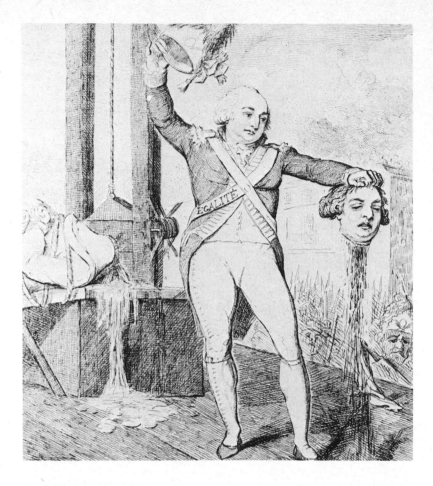

Philippe Egalité, Duc d'Orléans: Marie Antoinette's mortal enemy, who encouraged the flow of libellous tracts against her. He was also at the head of the freemasons' movement, as their Grand Master. A contemporary cartoon.

ceased to exist and was replaced by a Legislative Assembly of which Barnave was no longer a member. Suspected by the Jacobins, detested by the *émigrés*, his only hope was to return to Grenoble, his native province. As he kissed Marie Antoinette's hand in farewell, he remarked, 'I am sure to lose my head for interesting myself in your misfortunes and for the services which I have sought to render you.' Two years later he was guillotined.

On 29 September 1791, the new Assembly voted two decrees, the first ordering priests to take the civil oath at the risk of imprisonment should they refuse, and the second condemning the *émigrés* to death should they not return to France within two months. Louis vetoed both decrees. 'I do what everyone wants often enough for them to do what I want for once,' he said stubbornly, and the Revolution began to move once more. Matters were not improved when the Duc d'Orleans offered to help Louis

180

in his predicament only to be insulted in Marie Antoinette's drawing-room. One by one the other sovereigns turned their backs. A letter from Louis to Gustavus III explaining his acceptance of the Constitution was returned unopened, while Leopold II told his sister: 'There can be no question of using our gold or our blood in order to re-establish France in its former state.' 'What,' wrote Catherine of Russia, 'are we to think of persons who are continually championing two conflicting outlooks?' The Queen, Louis and Madame Elisabeth were continually arguing over the situation. To Fersen, Marie Antoinette wrote: 'My sister is so indiscreet, surrounded by schemers and held in leading-strings by her brothers across the frontier, that we find it impossible to converse with one another except at the risk of quarrelling from morning to night.' 'Our family life is hell,' she added. Each day, with the help of invisible ink and lemon juice, she wrote letters, which were sent to Brussels hidden in hats or biscuit boxes. 'I am exhausted with writing,' she said wearily. 'I have never worked so hard.'

To Fersen, the only possible solution was flight. On 13 February 1792, disguised as a courier and bearing forged papers, he returned to Paris at grave risk to his own life. That evening, he slipped into Marie Antoinette's apartments in the Tuileries by 'the usual route' and remained there for twenty-four hours before the Queen disclosed his presence to Louis. At six o'clock the following evening he went to see the King, who utterly refused to consider the idea of escaping. 'Louis is indeed a man of honour,' wrote Fersen sadly in his diary. At nine-thirty, unnoticed, he slipped out of the Tuileries. He had failed in his mission and it was the last time he was to see Marie Antoinette. Nine days later he left Paris. Within a week of his departure, Leopold, Marie Antoinette's faithless brother, unexpectedly died, shortly to be followed by Gustavus III, Fersen's main hope, who fell from an assassin's blow. War between France and Austria was now almost a certainty. Francis II, son of Leopold, was far more bellicose than his father, and in Paris Jacques Brissot and the Girondins were demanding battle.

The monarchy now had only four more months to live and in this short period of time it would squander its last great opportunity. General Dumouriez, whom the Gironde had forced Louis to appoint as Prime Minister, hoped to save the monarchy with his plans. But he reckoned without Marie Antoinette who, when he asked for an audience, haughtily informed him: 'Your existence is dependent on your conduct.' 'Neither the King nor I can bear all these innovations in the Constitution,' she added. Like Mira-beau, eighteen months before, he threw himself at her feet and kissed her hand. 'Allow yourself to be saved,' he begged her, but she would have none of it. 'One cannot believe in the protestations of a traitor,' she was to say to Madame Campan, thus spurning the support of one of the few men left who wished to help her.

War was now only a matter of days away, for Francis II had allowed the Prince de Condé to assemble an *émigré* army in the Austrian Netherlands. Marie Antoinette, full of hope for its success, betrayed her country by adoption and sent Mercy details of the French advance. On 20 April Louis was forced to propose to the Assembly 'a war against the King of Hungary and Bohemia'. As was to be expected, the French forces were put to rout, and by the end of the month Lafayette was suing for peace. While nothing could be proved against Marie Antoinette, her sympathies were evident and, with 'the Austrian committee', she was naturally accused. In the Manège, a few hundred yards from the garden front of the Tuileries, the Girondin Pierre Vergniaud declared he could 'see the home of false counsellors who misled the King and who forged chains for the French people, and who schemed to hand over the country to the Austrians'.

The Revolution now entered a more intense phase, and a series of decisive measures were passed by the Assembly. The constitu-tional guard, given to Louis some months before, was dismissed; the non-juring priests were to be deported; and a camp of twenty thousand Federates was set up in front of the walls of Paris. The King agreed only to the first, though the monarchy was thereby robbed of almost its last protection, but vetoed the two others, in spite of Dumouriez's urgent warning. No longer in harmony with his Girondin ministers, Louis XVI dismissed them, with the ex-ception of Dumouriez whom he tried to keep. But on 16 June, being unable to persuade the King to give way, the General pre-ferred to resign, and with him went the last defender of the monarchy.

On the evening of 19 June, three days later, Paris was in a fer-ment. Louis, with considerable misjudgment, had chosen the eve of the anniversary celebrations of the Oath of the Jeu de Paume to announce his veto on the decrees issued by the Legislative Assembly. All night long, the crowds gathered in the centre of the city. Pétion, now Mayor of Paris, chose to stay out of the way in the Hôtel de Ville. At eight the next morning, Terrier, Minister of the Interior, asserted that 'the night's news was not alarming',

The *Marseillaise*, battle-song
of the Revolutionaries. It
was composed by Rouget de
l'Isle and first heard in
April 1792 at the salon of
Madame Dietrich. It took its
title from the Marseillais
fédérés who sang it on their
march to Paris on 30 July 1792.

but an hour later he sent a message to the Directory, the governing
body of Paris, requesting troops to defend the Tuileries where the
gates were already closed. At ten o'clock the vast crowd, twenty
thousand strong, marched towards the Manège, where their leader
asked the Legislative Assembly why the army was idle, and if it
was on the King's orders, then he must go. 'The blood of patriots
must not be shed for the pride and ambition of the Tuileries.' Four
hours later, preceded by about ten musicians, according to an eye-
witness, there began the procession 'of citizens from all sections,
mingled with detachments of the National Guard and led by
Santerre and Saint-Huruge who was half-mad. The men were
armed with pikes, axes, paring-knives and sticks; some of the
women carried sabres.' They entered the grounds of the Tuileries
by the garden side, but then moved round to the Place du Carrousel.
By then it was four o'clock and Santerre had ordered the main
doors to be opened. The mob flooded in after him, dragging a
cannon behind them up the stairs to the first floor where they
installed it in the Oeil de Bœuf, the gallery which overlooked both
the courtyard and the garden.

183

Marie Antoinette and the faithful Madame de Lamballe, who had returned to be at her friend's side, rushed up the little staircase which led to the Dauphin's rooms, but already he had been taken to his sister. A few minutes later, the Queen was reunited with her children and together they went to hide in the little passage which separated the Dauphin's bedroom from the King's. Already the mob were breaking into the adjoining rooms. 'Marie Antoinette stifled her sobs,' recalled Madame de Tourzel. She knew nothing of her husband's fate until fifteen minutes later someone managed to reach her with the news that Louis xvi and his sister were in the Oeil de Bœuf, hemmed in on all sides by the rioters. The noise of the axes drew nearer all the time and when she heard the first door of the Dauphin's apartments being broken open, Marie Antoinette could bear it no longer. 'Let me go to the King, my duty calls me there.' In tears she went to face the mob, but she was stopped almost immediately by the Chevalier de Rougeville, a frequent visitor to the Tuileries. He led the whole party to the Council Room, which had not yet been broken into, and, protected by three rows of grenadiers drawn up in front of them, the little group sat behind a heavy table which had been dragged into the corner of the room.

In the Oeil de Bœuf the rioters were milling round the King demanding that he withdraw his veto, and threatening 'to come back every day'. Though he accepted every insult, even going so far as to put the red bonnet of liberty on his head, he still refused to yield. At six o'clock, Pétion finally made his appearance at the Tuileries, explaining that he had only just heard of the King's situation. Louis calmly pointed out that this had been going on for two hours. Hoisted on the shoulders of two grenadiers, the Mayor told the crowd they had behaved with 'the pride and dignity of free men', but now it was time for them to leave. Louis, by a master-stroke, turned the riotous mob into a party of peaceful sightseers, by suggesting that since they were in the palace, they might like to see the state apartments. As the door of the Council Room opened, there was general astonishment. Marie Antoinette, for whom they had searched everywhere, was sitting behind the table. Santerre ordered the grenadiers to divide, and the crowd saw the Queen take off the red cap of liberty which was placed on her head to put it on the Dauphin's head instead. She was acting wrongly, Santerre told her, but he would be responsible, none the less, for the people's good behaviour. 'See the Queen and the Royal Prince,' he shouted, as the long queue moved slowly past the table. It was 20 June, the first anniversary of the flight to Varennes. Very pale and with bloodshot eyes, Marie Antoinette held her head erect as she watched the ragged crowd file past, brandishing whips and carrying placards which read: '*À la lanterne!*' (literally 'Hang her up to the lamp-post' – 'Lynch her! String her up!') 'You're a vile woman,' one old hag shrieked. 'Have I ever done you any harm?' the Queen asked her quietly. Madame Elisabeth had joined the line as the only way to reach her sister-in-law. 'The King is safe,' she said, as she passed Marie Antoinette. It was the first news she had had for the past three hours. By eight that evening the last of the rioters had gone from the Tuileries, leaving a trail of broken glass and smashed doors behind them. Louis XVI was at last able to join his family. As he entered the room, he was still wearing the red bonnet that the rioters had put upon his head.

Madame Manon Roland, painted by Madame Labille-Guiard. Determined to play some part in the Revolution, she fomented hatred for the Girondins in her salon.

'I still exist, but it is by a miracle,' wrote Marie Antoinette to Fersen. Daily, the rumours were becoming more sinister and 'the band of assassins grows constantly larger'. Madame Campan had a bodice made for her mistress which would 'resist knife thrusts and bullets' but she refused to wear it: 'If the insurgents assassinate me it will be a blessing; they will deliver me from a most miserable existence.' At night she continued to sleep unguarded though once, at least, a suspicious figure had appeared in her bedroom. She had stopped walking in the gardens of the Tuileries to avoid hearing the constant refrain of the popular song:

> *Madame Veto avait promis*
> *De faire égorger tout Paris.*
> [Madame Veto had promised
> To butcher all Paris.]

The chapel orchestra took to playing '*Ça ira*', the most chilling of the Revolution's songs, and under the Queen's windows passers-by were able to buy indecent engravings showing Marie Antoinette lying in the arms of Madame de Polignac, the Princesse de Lamballe or the Comte d'Artois. Soon, she was not able to sleep at all. 'She insisted that the shutters and blinds should not be closed', wrote Madame Campan, 'so that her long, sleepless nights might be less trying.'

The horror of the last days is reflected in the Queen's letters to Fersen. 'Ours is a dreadful situation . . . time presses and it is impossible to wait longer.' 'Tell Monsieur de Mercy', she wrote, 'that the lives of the King and Queen are in the greatest danger,

185

Holland.

Savoy.

Vive la Liberty

Germany & Prussia

Italy.

John Bull.

Sans-Culottes, feeding Europe
with the Bread of Liberty—

Pub. Jan 30 1793 by H Humphrey No 18 Old Bond Street

A contemporary English cartoon: the French Revolutionaries are shown stirring up trouble in the other European countries by feeding them 'the Bread of Liberty'. The French Revolution did, indeed, spark off movements elsewhere.

that one day's delay may produce incalculable misfortune, that the manifesto must be sent at once and it is awaited with extreme impatience.' For a long time Marie Antoinette had been asking the allies to issue this manifesto, her idea being to draw a clear distinction between the cause of republicanism and that of the French nation. Above all, she urged that the foreign powers must carefully avoid interfering with the internal concerns of France. 'Be careful', she said, 'not to say too much about the King, and not to arouse the impression that your main purpose is to give him support.' But on 25 July, when the Duke of Brunswick proclaimed the Manifesto at Coblenz, he threatened Paris with military force 'if the least violence or the least outrage is committed against their Majesties the King and Queen'. It contained all the errors which the Queen, better informed, had hoped to avoid, with the result

186

that even those who till now had been loyal to the King, became ardent republicans. The allied threat to raze Paris to the ground should the Tuileries be stormed, was taken by the populace as a valid reason to attack.

Preparations began almost immediately. Danton, Robespierre and the Girondists were swiftly and silently issuing orders to an illegal army, the people of Paris, as they waited for the arrival of six hundred Reds from Marseilles. On 6 August they marched into Paris in time to a new marching song, the *Marseillaise*, which would soon become the battle-cry of the Revolution.

On the night of 9 to 10 August, no one was asleep in the Tuileries. At quarter to one in the morning the call to arms began to sound from a distant suburb. By half-past two all the churches in Paris were answering the signal given by Danton from the Church of the Cordeliers. Guarding the château was the Swiss Regiment of nine hundred men who had been summoned from Courbevoie, the National Guard, of questionable loyalty, and the Royalist battalion of the Filles Saint-Thomas. Altogether, they could count on a force of fifteen hundred. Marie Antoinette, followed by the Princesse de Lamballe, wandered from room to room, watching from the balconies for signs of movement. At one point Madame Elisabeth called to her: 'My sister, come and watch the dawn break.' It was four o'clock. The sky was blood-red. All of a sudden, the tocsin ended, but the relief they all felt was entirely unmerited, for that moment the Tuileries was losing its only defender. The Marquis de Mandat, Commander of the National Guard, had just been brutally murdered on the steps of the Hôtel de Ville and his body sent floating down the Seine.

The suburbs began to make their way towards the Tuileries. Urged on by his wife, Louis went down to review the forces and put some heart into the defence, while from a window Marie Antoinette watched the scene. Nothing less stirring could be imagined than the few ill-chosen words with which the King addressed these men who had been ready to die for him. Instead of diminishing their insecurity, he only helped to increase it. A great shout of 'Long live the Nation!' drowned the applause of the Swiss Guards, and soon there were open cries of revolt: '*A bas le veto! A bas le gros cochon!*' ('Down with the veto! Down with the fat pig!') 'Good God! It's the King they are reviling,' said the Minister for the Navy, horrified, who had been watching from the first floor. Marie Antoinette, her eyes red-rimmed from weeping, and worn out by the sleepless night, turned away in despair.

The capture of the Tuileries, which ushered in the final stage of imprisonment
for the royal family. An engraving after Prieur.

To Madame Campan, she said: 'All is lost. This review of troops has done more harm than good.'

By now it was seven in the morning and the vanguard of the rebels had arrived, a disorderly and imperfectly trained crowd, but single-minded in their determination. Roederer, the Public Prosecutor, keenly alive to his responsibilities, had urged the King an hour before to take himself to the National Assembly, and put himself under the protection of the Deputies. Marie Antoinette had interposed, saying coldly: 'Monsieur, we have a strong enough force here, and it is time to decide which shall have the upper hand, the King and the Constitution, or the rebels.' But, by now, Roederer was insistent: 'Sir, your Majesty has not five minutes to lose. You will find safety only in the National Assembly.' 'But I did not see many people in the Carrousel,' the unhappy man stammered. 'Monsieur,' said Marie Antoinette, 'we have troops.' 'Madame, all Paris is marching.' 'The King raised his head,' wrote Roederer, 'looked fixedly at me for a few seconds, then, turning to the Queen, he said: "Let us go" and rose.'

Surrounded by a body of National Guards, the King led the way. Behind him, Marie Antoinette, 'red and weeping', held her son by the hand and was followed by Madame Royale, Madame Elisabeth, the Princesse de Lamballe, Madame de Tourzel, the Ministers and a handful of faithful supporters. 'We shall soon be back,' Marie Antoinette called back to Monsieur de Jarjayes. Clinging to his mother's hand, the Dauphin amused himself, as they walked through the garden, by kicking the leaves at the legs of the people walking in front of him. At the Assembly, the President greeted the royal family with the words: 'You can count, Sire, on the firmness of the National Assembly,' before shutting them into a little office behind his chair. Pedantically, they were following the clause in the Constitution which forbade the King to be present when the Assembly was actually in session. This tiny box, normally used by newspaper reporters, was less than twelve feet square; its ceiling was so low that a full-grown man could not stand upright. Up to now, an iron grating had separated it from the hall of the Assembly, but, fearing an attack from the mob, it was broken down to enable the Deputies to reach the royal family should the worst happen. Squashed together until ten that evening, the royal family had no recourse but to listen to the debate on the future of the monarchy. Marie Antoinette sat expressionless, her face to the wall, while the children tried fitfully to sleep. The King seemed quite at his ease. In the distance, the sound of gunfire died away, signal-

The Temple: there the royal family occupied the middle storeys. A contemporary engraving.

ling that the château had at last surrendered. In front of the Queen's eyes, the rioters began to bring their spoils into the hall: her jewels, silver, letters found on her table, and boxes of her correspondence.

No longer were the deputies masters of the debate; the Commune, Robespierre, Marat and Danton now insisted that matters be settled. At the beginning of the afternoon, Vergniaud rose, and speaking of the 'grief' with which his colleagues were filled, he asked for the immediate adoption of two measures: 'The French people is invited to form a National Convention. . . . The head of the Executive Power is provisionally suspended from his functions.' That evening the royal family, the Princesse de Lamballe, Madame de Tourzel and one of the Queen's women, Madame Augié, were placed in the little cells of the Feuillant convent next to the Manège. No one slept. At the end of the corridor, behind a

190

grille, a mad crowd shouted threats of death. 'When one of the ladies appeared at the door of the apartment,' wrote an eye witness, 'she was obliged by the terrifying crowds to return at once. Every time I looked through the grille I thought I was in a menagerie watching the fury of the wild beasts when someone approaches the bars.'

At seven-thirty on Saturday morning, 11 August, the royal family were led again to the little Press box. Throughout the day they were forced to listen to speeches, each more republican than the last, while there were discussions as to how to prevent the King from being carried off. The following day, the question of their future residence began in earnest; but it was not until evening that Manuel suggested putting them in the Temple. Pétion did not dare tell the King that he was to live not in the former palace of the Comte d'Artois but in the tower which stood in the gardens of the Temple, only a hundred yards away. The keep, about sixty feet high, was a gloomy stronghold, four-square and sinister with round towers at the corners, narrow windows and a sunless inner court. To lodge the prisoners, ceilings would have to be built and the rooms divided by partitions. Meanwhile, Manuel decided to confine the royal family in 'the little tower', a more modern construction backing on to the keep.

At six o'clock on the evening of 13 August the royal family started on a journey that was to take them two hours through the crowded streets to reach the palace of the Temple in the north-east corner of the city. In the Salle des Graces, where the Comte d'Artois had formerly received Marie Antoinette, they had to sit down and make a pretence of eating. Towards one in the morning, having learned that they were not to stay there, Marie Antoinette and the royal party crossed the torch-lit garden towards the entrance to the tall tower. All evening the guards had been singing a song with the constant refrain:

> Madame mont à sa tour
> Ne sait quand descendra.
> [Madame goes up her tower
> Knowing not when she will descend.]

On the first floor she found her son who had fallen asleep over his supper. Madame de Tourzel had carried him over a short while before. She was not to descend from her tower for nearly a year.

8 Descent from the Tower 1792-3

OVER THE NEXT FEW WEEKS the Temple defences were strengthened still further. An additional rampart was built and, to clear the approaches, a number of small houses near the tower were demolished and trees cut down in the courtyard below. Guardrooms were established at every exit and new barriers set up in the passages within to ensure that anyone entering or leaving the Temple would run the gauntlet of seven or eight sentries. Each day, four Commissaries of the Commune, chosen by lot, checked every room of the fortress and at night took charge of the keys of every door.

Late on the evening of 19 August came the order from the Commune that 'any persons who did not actually form part of the family of Capet' must at once leave the Temple. Full of grief at parting from the loyal Princesse de Lamballe, Marie Antoinette drew Madame de Tourzel aside as the two left for the prison of La Force and implored her to look after her friend. 'Take care of Lamballe,' she begged. 'Speak for her if you can and see that she has no awkward questions to answer.' Only too well aware of the Lamballe's inadequacies, she was trying at the last moment to protect her vulnerable friend. Of the former retinue, now only Hue, the King's valet, remained, shortly to be joined by Cléry, who had been valet to the Dauphin. For the rougher work the Commune had employed a man named Tison, who, with his domineering wife, was to keep a close watch on the royal captives.

The Commune, at first, was not ungenerous in its efforts to bring relative comfort to the prisoners' lives. Space was fairly limited as there were only five rooms in the little tower, but the Queen and her son slept adequately enough on the second floor in two rooms divided by a closet. The King had been installed on the floor above, while the rest of the party disposed themselves as best they could. In food and drink, the matters on which Louis's comfort mainly depended, the Commune was particularly liberal, and menus, which still exist, show that they ate often more lavishly in the Temple than they had done at the Tuileries. At the main meal, no less than three soups were presented, four *entrées*, six roasts and four or five desserts, not to mention the *compôtes* and fruit that came later. To drink there was malmsey, claret and champagne, and while in the evening two of the *entrées* were withdrawn, the number of roasts and desserts was the same. They were given, too, an abundant supply of clothing. Very little had been salvaged from the Tuileries and Marie Antoinette was allowed by the Commune to order what seems a substantial enough ward-

PREVIOUS PAGES Marie Antoinette bids farewell to her children, watched by the guards waiting to take her to the Conciergerie. Madame Elisabeth is also shown in this contemporary artist's impression.

194

robe for such straitened circumstances. Thirty dressmakers set to work for 'the former Queen' and tradesmen were soon delivering coats of Florence taffeta in 'Paris mud' colour, fichus, lawn bonnets, shoes of puce, blue or grey, lawn sashes for 'coat-dresses', Chinese *sabots* and caps in black beaver. Louis's request for books was similarly granted. Over 250 arrived, and while the King found consolation in French and Latin literature, Marie Antoinette and her sister-in-law found a lighter relief in romances and novels such as *A Thousand and One Nights* or Fanny Burney's *Evelina*.

Slowly, their life assumed a pattern. At nine o'clock the whole family would assemble in the King's room for breakfast, after which they would go down to Marie Antoinette's room where they spent most of the day. The morning was devoted mainly to the children's lessons. The King would make his son recite passages from Corneille and Racine, give him geography lessons and teach him to draw maps, while Marie Antoinette supervised her daughter's drawing and needlework. If it was fine outside, they would go down to the Temple garden where Louis and Cléry would play ball with the little Dauphin. An hour later they would return to the Tower for lunch and then spend the long afternoon playing piquet or backgammon, resting or making general conversation. Supper was at nine, after which Louis would retire to his study, leaving the rest of his family to go to bed.

Had it not been for the constant supervision to which they were subjected, their life, though monotonous, would have seemed relatively peaceful. At table, their bread rolls were prodded to see that they contained no secret messages, and even the children's lessons were regarded with deep suspicion. The Dauphin's multiplication tables, thought to be an elaborate system for breaking code, were confiscated, while the guards seized on Madame Royale's drawings of Roman emperors' heads, imagining them to be portraits of the Allied leaders who were combining against France. But, by degrees, their hostility lessened when they found their prisoners not to be the tyrants they had imagined. Even Goret, a municipal guard often on duty at the Temple, who at first had made a particular point of irritating Louis with the title of 'Capet', now came to show sympathy to the captives. Often he would be left alone with the Queen, for, too proud to expose herself needlessly to the mockery of the sentinels, she would sometimes stay behind in her room to work at her sewing while the King and Dauphin tried to fly their kite in the garden below. One day she showed the guard some little twists of paper in which she

195

The royal prisoners are
served a meal in the Temple.

had kept her children's hair at different ages. 'The Queen put them back where she had taken them', he related, 'and came back to me rubbing scent into her hands and passing them before my face so that I could smell the scent which had a very sweet perfume.'

If life seemed calm enough within the Temple, outside, the Republic was fighting for its life. Hébert, the Deputy Public Prosecutor, who once a week paid deferential visits to the Temple, was all the time building resistance to the Allied threat by whipping up public opinion against the royal prisoners in his scurrilous journal, *Père Duchesne*. No newspapers were allowed in the quadrangle of the Temple for fear the prisoners should learn of news from abroad, and it was only thanks to Turgy, a serving-lad who had been in the kitchens of the Tuileries, that they were kept aware of events. The code that Marie Antoinette gave him shows how much hope she still had. From the way he placed his fingers on his face she would know if the Austrian troops had won a victory. 'When they are fifteen leagues from Paris the fingers will be carried to the mouth.'

On 3 September, Louis was standing at the window of his room watching the demolition of one of the houses close by. Though the Temple defences were thereby being strengthened, he was laughing loudly as the pieces of stone and wood fell to the ground. 'His pleasure was brief,' recalls Daujon, Commissioner of the Commune, who was standing beside him. 'The loud report of a gun checked it; a second report quenched it; a third replaced it with terror. It was the alarm gun.' The Duke of Brunswick had at last invaded France and already Verdun had capitulated. From Cléry, the royal family learned only 'that there was a commotion in Paris' and that 'the people were going to the prisons'. Paris, in the event of a life or death struggle, was taking no chances from traitors in the city. The killing went on all night. By the time the September massacres were over, between eleven hundred and fourteen hundred people had been dragged from the prisons and murdered in cold blood.

The following day, the royal family still knew nothing of what had happened until a piercing cry suddenly reached them from below. A few seconds later Cléry burst into the room, speechless, his eyes full of horror. Framed in the downstairs window he had just seen the severed head of the Princesse de Lamballe. The night before, she had been brought out of La Force and horribly mutilated, and the crowd, having dragged her naked body to the

Je suis le véritable père Duchesne, foutre!

LA GRANDE JOIE
DU
PERE DUCHESNE,

DE voir que la convention donne le coup de grace aux accapareurs, aux affameurs du peuple, aux muscadins et muscadines. Sa grande colère de ce que les grands intrigans et les gros fripons sont épargnés. Ses bons avis aux braves montagnards pour qu'ils fassent déclarer suspects tous les jean-foutres qui étoient les amis de Brissot, et qui taupoient dans le fédéralisme avant le 31 mai.

LE compère Audouin, brave montagnard, et journaliste de mon acabie, qui écrit pour

292.

OPPOSITE Parisian
Revolutionaries, 1793–4:
(left to right) a member of
the Commune; a gaoler at
the Temple; a henchman of
the Comités, and a soldier.
From contemporary prints.

Temple, were now calling for the Queen to kiss the head of her whore. Still unaware of what was going on, Marie Antoinette begged to know what was being hidden from her. By now the room was full of municipal officers; one of them, despite Cléry's entreaties, explained to her 'in the coarsest possible tones: "They want to hide from you the head of the Lamballe which has been brought here to show you how the people takes its revenge on tyrants"'. 'Frozen with horror', Marie Antoinette fainted without a sound. It was the only time her daughter ever saw her lose her sense of firmness. 'My aunt and I heard them beating the call to arms all night,' wrote the fifteen-year-old child. 'My poor mother could not sleep all night. It was only later that we learned that the massacre had lasted three days.' On 20 September, the Duke of Brunswick's advance was checked. At Valmy the French scored an overwhelming victory and the Prussian armies were forced to retreat across the border. Two days later, Louis XVI was formally deposed. Their very existence threatened, the French were now on an all-out attack. Savoy and Nice were occupied, and along the Rhine the cities of Spier, Worms and Mainz fell to the revolutionary armies.

Though cut off from the outside world, news of what was happening still found its way into the Temple. Turgy would stop the decanters with bits of paper on which were written 'advice and news in lemon juice or an extract made from gall-nuts'. Notes would be hidden in the Princesses' beds in reels of cotton or rolled round lead pellets dropped into a bottle of almond milk.

On 26 September came the news that Louis was to be transferred to the great tower of the Temple. Rooms had been prepared for him on the second floor, where shuttered windows allowed the light to enter from above but made it impossible to see in or out. Even the shoemaker Simon, one of the most repellent figures of the Revolution, was moved as he witnessed the separation. 'I do believe', he was heard to mutter, 'that these women will end by making me shed tears too.' A month later the whole family were reunited in the great tower. As Marie Antoinette was transferred to her new rooms above the King's, she was forced twelve times to stoop through the wicket gates that guarded the winding stair while on each landing, heavy doors with bolts and chains divided the staircase from the rooms themselves.

The father, wife and sister were together less frequently [wrote Goret, noting the sinking morale of the prisoners]. It seemed they feared to increase their misfortunes by talking about them. The children had lost

their playfulness they had maintained till then. The King walked to and fro and wandered from his room into the other one where we were sitting. The Queen sat in her room more quietly, but Madame Elizabeth walked to and fro like the King and often had a book in her hand.

On 7 December an added precaution was taken. All scissors, knives and razors were taken away from the prisoners. The King had to hand over his toothpick and even his tinder-box, while Marie Antoinette and the princesses were given back only the few small things that were absolutely necessary for their sewing. Even forks were allowed on the sole condition that they would be removed immediately after use.

Four days later, Louis was removed from the Temple. On 20 November the King's private papers had been discovered in a secret cupboard in the Tuileries and had brought to light Mirabeau's double-dealings and Lafayette's obvious royalist sympathies. Both discoveries gave the Commune its long-awaited pretext on which to charge Louis and bring him to trial at the bar of the Assembly.

In the Temple the Dauphin was moved up to his mother's bedroom. It was to be six weeks before Marie Antoinette would see her husband once more. Cléry and Turgy in the meantime brought her news, and Toulan, the fierce Republican Commissioner who none the less had rallied to her cause, had bribed a paper-seller to shout his daily news within earshot of her window. On Sunday 20 January 1793, her last hopes were shattered as she heard his stentorian voice below, announcing that the National Convention had decreed the death penalty upon her husband: 'The execution shall take place within twenty-four hours of its notification to the prisoner.'

That evening, for the last time, the condemned man was allowed to see his family. Cléry, who could see but not hear through the glass-panelled door of the dining-room, left the following account:

It was half-past eight in the evening. Marie Antoinette appeared first, holding her son's hand and followed by Madame Royale and Madame Elisabeth. They all threw themselves into the King's arms. For a few minutes the silence was only broken by the sounds of sobs. This painful scene lasted one hour and three quarters during which it was impossible to hear anything; through a glass door we only saw that after every sentence of the King's, the princesses' sobs increased and that the King then gave up trying to speak.

OPPOSITE The last letter that Louis wrote before his execution. In it he asked the National Convention for three days' grace, to prepare for his death, but this was refused.

202

20 janvier 1793.

Je demande ~~à la Convention Nationale~~ un delai de trois jours pour
pouvoir me preparer a paroitre devant la presence de Dieu. je
demande pour cela de pouvoir voir *librement* la personne que j'indiquerai aux
commissaires de la Commune, et que cette personne soit a l'abri de toute
inquietude et crainte *de toute* pour cet Acte de Charité qu'elle remplira auprès de
moi. je demande ~~à la Convention Nationale~~ d'estre delivré de la
surveillance perpetuelle que le Conseil General a etabli depuis quelques
jours.

Je demande dans cet intervalle a *pouvoir* voir ma famille quand je le
~~demanderai~~ et sans ~~temoins~~ temoins. je desirerois bien que la Convention
Nationale s'occupat tout de suite du sort de ma famille, et qu'elle lui
permit de se retirer librement et convenablement ou elle le jugeroit a
propos.

Je recommende à la bienfaisance de la Nation toutes les personnes qui
m'étoient attachées, il y en a beaucoup qui avoient mis toute leur
fortune dans leurs charges, et qui n'ayant plus d'appointements
doivent estre dans le besoin, et même de celles qui ne vivoient que
de leurs appointements. Dans les pensionaires il y a beaucoup de
vieillards de femmes et d'enfants qui n'avoient que cela pour vivre.

a la Tour du Temple le Janvier 1793.

Louis

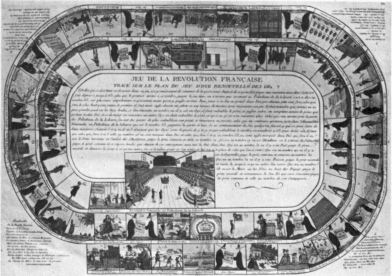

ABOVE J. Bertaux's painting of the taking of the Tuileries on 10 August 1792.

BELOW The Game of Goose – the French Revolution (1790-1). Other board games known as 'The Game of Goose' took as their theme the 'Cries of Paris'.

At a quarter past ten Louis rose and when Cléry entered he saw Marie Antoinette holding her husband's arm and 'uttering cries of the deepest grief'. 'I assure you', said Louis, 'that I shall see you tomorrow at eight.' 'Why not at seven?' begged Marie Antoinette. 'Very well, yes, at seven,' Louis replied, knowing full well that he would never see them again.

On the floor below, the guards still heard the sound of sobbing as Marie Antoinette threw herself fully dressed on to her bed. 'We heard her all through the night, trembling with cold and grief,' wrote Madame Royale. At five o'clock the following morning she heard Cléry lighting the fire in the King's bedroom above. An hour later the door of her room opened, but it was only an officer who had come to borrow Madame Elisabeth's missal for the condemned man's Mass. At nine the trumpets sounded as Louis crossed the garden, but above, the family could see nothing through their shuttered windows. They heard only voices and the sound of departing footsteps. An hour and a half later there was a sudden cry of 'Long live the Republic!', and the drums of the sentry guards began to beat in unison below the windows of the keep. Marie Antoinette understood what had just happened. 'She choked with grief', related Turgy, 'and the young prince burst into tears.' A few minutes later she saluted him as King.

Unable to bear the thought of passing her husband's door, she now refused to go down to the garden and instead would sit at the top of the tower where a parapet surrounded the circular gallery. Her only mementoes were those which the King had entrusted to Cléry shortly before his execution: his seal with the arms of France, his wedding ring used in the proxy marriage in Vienna, and locks of all his family's hair. These had been confiscated by the Commune and set under seal, but Toulan, at great risk, had stolen them back for her.

It was he who, with Jarjayes, now formulated a plan for escape. Toulan and Lepître, a sympathetic member of the Provisional Commune, were to smuggle in articles of men's clothing to disguise the Queen and Madame Elisabeth, while the young Louis and Madame Royale were to escape as the two ragged children of the lamplighter who every evening made his rounds at five-thirty. The Tisons would be drugged by their favourite Spanish tobacco, thus leaving them unconscious for several hours. Everything was ready except for the passports, which were Lepître's province, but at the crucial moment Dumouriez defected to the Allies and, as a result, no more passports were to be issued. Lepître hesitated and the whole plot collapsed. It would still have been possible to save the Queen, but Marie Antoinette, rather than abandon her children, refused to think of the idea. 'We have dreamed a beautiful dream, nothing more,' she wrote to Jarjayes as he made his way back to the frontier. But to his safekeeping she entrusted the ring and the seal, her last treasures, to be delivered to the Comte de Provence. At the same time she sent him a wax impression made from the ring Fersen had given her at their last parting. 'I want you to give it to the person whom you know to have come to see me from Brussels last winter and to tell him at the same time that the motto has never been more true.' It showed a pigeon in full flight surrounded by the words: '*Tutto a te mi guida*' ('Everything leads me to you').

Not only Fersen wished for her escape. A little later, the Baron de Batz, who had already tried to save the King between the Temple and the scaffold, formed another plot. With the complicity of Michonis, the prison administrator, he planned to lead his men into the Temple, give the prisoners military hats and cloaks and, surrounding them by his patrol, march them out of prison. At midnight on 21-22 June, Batz and his men were already waiting in the street, when Simon, one of the Commissaries of the Commune, burst in. He had just received, anonymously, a note which read: 'Beware, Michonis will betray you tonight.' But, as Batz managed to slip away into the night, no one was implicated, as Michonis was able to convince everyone it had been a false alarm.

Two plans of escape had failed and the prisoners now seemed to hold out less hope of rescue. The two women played at Republican cards while Louis continued his lessons. 'It is impossible not to be touched by the sight of the little King', wrote Lepître, 'bending over his little table, reading the history of France with the greatest attention, then repeating what he had read and listening eagerly to the observations of his mother and aunt. But their sympathizers were soon to be rooted out. Tison's wife, never to be trusted, finally denounced Toulan, Lepître and all the officers who had 'truckled to the widow Capet'. When she learned on 29 June that the Committee of Public Safety had decided to remove the little King from his mother, she became full of remorse. Throwing herself at the prisoners' feet, she begged wildly for forgiveness, screaming and falling into convulsions at the same time. The next day eight men carried her shrieking from the tower. She had gone raving mad. Marie Antoinette understood the significance only when, on 3 July, four days later, six officials of the Commune entered her room late

206

The execution of Louis on 21 January 1793. According to royalist legend, he addressed these words to the waiting crowd: 'People, I die an innocent man! I forgive those responsible for my death and I pray God that my blood will not fall upon France.'

at night to bring her the news. From now on her son was to occupy
the rooms below that once had been Louis XVI's, with the horrible
Simon as his 'tutor'. The child, who by now had woken up, threw
himself sobbing into his mother's arms, begging to stay. 'An hour
went by in discussions, in insults and threats from all the officers,
in pleading and tears from all of us,' recalls Madame Royale. 'Finally
my mother consented to give up her son. We got him up and when
he was dressed my mother handed him over to the officers, bathing

him in tears as though she knew she would never see him again. The poor little boy embraced us all tenderly and went out weeping with the men.'

For hours on end, Marie Antoinette would now watch from a little window in one of the towers 'to see her son pass at a distance when his guardian led him to the roof of the tower'. Already Simon's education was having a coarsening effect on his pupil. Hébert had advised him to turn the 'whelp' into a perfect patriot and slowly the little boy was being terrorized into forgetting his past loyalties. From her room above, Marie Antoinette could hear him singing the *Ça ira*, the *Carmagnole* and the *Marseillaise* at the top of his voice. 'I was playing a game of bowls with him one day', related Daujon, 'the room where we were was below one of the family's rooms and we could hear a sound like jumping and chairs being moved over our heads, which made quite a lot of noise. The child thereupon said with an impatient gesture: "Haven't those damn whores been guillotined yet?"' Only a few weeks before, this little King of eight had wept inconsolably on being separated from his mother.

Outside the Temple walls, the Republic was in greater danger than ever before and the Revolution, still dominated by Danton and Robespierre, therefore entered its most extreme phase. On 28 July, the great fortress of Valenciennes, where Fersen's regiment had formerly been stationed, fell to the Allies. The road to the Capitol was now open. In Brussels, Fersen was forming a plan 'to drive with a large force of cavalry towards Paris, which would be all the easier since there was no army ahead and all the barns were full of provisions'. In an attempt to stay the Allied advance, the revolutionaries now hoped to use the Queen's life as a bargaining tactic by making the foreign powers believe she was to be brought to trial. Unanimously on 1 August the Convention voted to refer 'the widow Capet' to the Revolutionary Tribunal. Very late that night, four police administrators headed by Michonis came to read to Marie Antoinette the decree transferring her to the Conciergerie.

By now she seemed immune to all suffering, as quietly and 'without emotion' she prepared a parcel of clothes with the help of her daughter and Madame Elisabeth. In front of the police officers who watched her as she dressed, she 'showed her pockets'. After searching her, they left her only a handkerchief and a bottle of smelling salts 'in case she felt ill'. The rest they packed up. She embraced her daughter, entrusting her to Madame Elisabeth's

208

care, and left the room quickly without looking back at either. As she left the tower, she hit her head sharply as she forgot to stoop at the final wicket gate. 'Did you hurt yourself?' Michonis asked anxiously. 'Oh no,' she answered. 'Nothing can hurt me any more.' Surrounded by twenty *gendarmes* who rode beside her, the Queen drove away from the Temple in a small carriage, which twenty minutes later drew up in the Cours de Mai outside the Palais de Justice. Below the Palais was the Conciergerie where she was to be taken. Larivière, one of the eight turnkeys, was still full of sleep when he answered the knocking on the prison door, and opening it, he saw through the darkness of the night, a 'tall, beautiful woman' surrounded by men in uniform. As she entered the room, he recognized Marie Antoinette, 'dressed in a long black garment which made her extraordinary whiteness even more dazzling'.

Her new prison was a cell, dripping with damp, and lit by a low window almost level with the ground of the women's courtyard. It had quickly been furnished that afternoon by Madame Richard, the wife of the concierge, who, assisted by Rosalie Lamorlière, had installed a camp-bed, two mattresses, a bolster, a blanket, a cane armchair to put clothes on and 'a red leather basin with its spray, all new, for the use of the said Widow Capet'. In the small, low room, crowded with people, Marie Antoinette wiped the sweat away from her forehead. She watched Richard enter her name in the Register, his 280th prisoner, 'accused of having conspired against France', and put her seal to the packet of her belongings removed from the Temple. Finally, she was alone, except for Rosalie who came forward shyly and offered to help the prisoner. 'Thank you, my girl,' she replied, 'but now that I have no one I serve myself.'

In hastening Marie Antoinette's trial, the Revolutionaries had vastly overestimated her bargaining power. The monarchs of Europe were far more interested in saving their own countries from Republicanism than in rescuing a fallen Queen of France. 'There is nothing to do but wait,' said Mercy philosophically, when the news reached Brussels, and Fersen's scheme of invasion was abandoned. His grief was slight. He had never liked his 'ward', and besides, was hardly likely to take advice from the Queen's lover, the one man he had never been able to forgive. Fersen, on the other hand, was distraught: 'I am no longer living', he wrote to his sister Sophie, 'for it is not living to exist as I do and to suffer such grief. . . . If I could only still act to deliver her I feel that I

209

should suffer less, but to be able to do nothing but entreat, is agony for me.'

Larivière's eighty-year-old mother came at first, to wait upon the Queen. Her son was immediately despatched to buy 'half an ell of muslin' to patch the prisoner's dress which was 'in holes under the arms and worn at the hem'. Four days later she was replaced by the 'Citizen Harel', who the Queen did not seem to care for so much. On the day Madame Harel began her duties, the Administrators confiscated the little gold watch Marie Antoinette had brought from Vienna twenty-three years before. She wept bitterly now, at its loss. Two other people were forced on her: Gilbert, a 'National *gendarme*' and his superior, Sergeant François Dufresne. Until 13 September they lived in the same room, only $11\frac{1}{2}$ feet square, which was divided in two by a screen so that the Queen could dress in privacy.

At seven o'clock she would rise, put on her little 'turned-down' slippers and drink a cup of coffee or chocolate. She dressed by a little mirror which Rosalie had lent her. 'It made me blush', she said, 'to offer it for I had bought the mirror on the quays and it only cost twenty-five *sous*. It was edged with red and had chinese faces painted on each side of it.' 'Her hair was very simply dressed,' the servant related. 'She parted it in the front after putting on a little scented powder. Madame Harel bound the ends of her hair with a piece of white ribbon, knotted it firmly and then handed the ends to Madame, who, by tying them herself and pinning them on top of her head, arranged her hair in the form of a loose chignon.' Thanks to Michonis, Marie Antoinette had sent from the Temple some chemises 'trimmed with lace known as mignonettes', two pairs of black silk stockings, a mantle, three lawn fichus and, most important, a pair of shoes *à la Saint-Huberty*. The ones she had were already falling to pieces with the damp. She was also able to get a box of powder and a puff. To keep these treasures from getting dusty, Rosalie lent her a cardboard box which she received 'with as much satisfaction as if she had been lent the most beautiful piece of furniture in the world'.

Her food, too, was prepared with care by Madame Richard: soup, boiled beef, a dish of vegetables, chicken or duck – her favourite dish, and a dessert. In the evening she would have cutlets, beef and a *fricassée* of turkey or pigeon, while she drank only Ville d'Avray water which came every day from the Temple.

After supper, her only distraction was to lean on the back of a chair and watch the two *gendarmes* playing backgammon.

The young Louis XVII, hope of the royalists, playing with a yo-yo: by Madame Vigée-Lebrun. He was fated to die only two years after his parents.

Condemned to inactivity she would, from time to time, pull out coarse threads from the canvas covering of the walls, and with a hairpin 'made very plain lace, using her knee as a cushion'. She now read, with keen interest, *The Travels of Captain Cook*, *A Voyage to Venice* and *A History of Famous Shipwrecks*, confiding to Richard 'that she read with pleasure the most terrifying adventures'. She got into the habit of playing with her two solitaire rings which the prison authorities had forgotten to take away. 'Without her realizing it', wrote Rosalie, 'these two jewels were a kind of toy for her. As she sat and mused she would take them off, put them on again, and pass them from one hand to another, several times in one minute.'

211

To distract her, Madame Richard one day brought her youngest child to see the Queen. Marie Antoinette, according to Rosalie,

> seeing this handsome little boy, started visibly. She took him in her arms, covered him with kisses and caresses and began to cry, while she spoke to us of Monsieur le Dauphin who was about the same age. . . . Hidden in her bodice she wore the portrait of the young King and a lock of his hair wrapped in a little yellow glove which had belonged to the child, and I noticed that she often concealed herself near her wretched camp-bed to kiss these objects as she wept.

Her evident distress began to soften those who had intended to be severe jailers. Gilbert and Dufresne, her two guards, rough though they were, often brought flowers to their prisoner which they themselves had paid for, while the police administrators, Michonis and Jobert, would occasionally bring visitors to see her, such as a certain Mademoiselle Fouché who had managed to bribe the warders into allowing her to bring the Abbé Magnin, a non-juring priest, in her charitable visits to the prisons. With the connivance of her keepers, Marie Antoinette was therefore able to make her confession and receive Holy Communion.

On 28 August the Queen saw Michonis enter her cell with a man whose 'clothes were spattered with the mud of Paris'. Almost immediately 'her face was aflame' as she recognized the Chevalier de Rougeville, the same man who had led her to safety during the demonstrations at the Tuileries on 20 June of the previous year. He now stepped towards her, and taking two carnations from his buttonhole, he threw them down by the stove. In spite of his 'meaning look' she stared blankly at him until, drawing a little closer, he managed to whisper to her to pick up the note. He then left. With astonishing presence of mind, Marie Antoinette asked Gilbert, then on duty, to take a complaint about her food and, as soon as his back was turned, she picked up the two flowers and saw that each had a note. One assured her of de Rougeville's loyalty and asked her if she wanted three or four hundred *louis* for bribes, while the other apparently contained 'a safe and well thought-out plan for her escape if she wished to lend herself to it'. Quarter of an hour later, when de Rougeville returned with Michonis, she gave him an affirmative answer. He promised to return in two days time with the money for bribes. Immediately he had gone, Marie Antoinette decided to try to enlist Gilbert's help. Before de Rougeville's return on the Friday, she had managed to prick out with a pin a message to be delivered to him by Gilbert.

OPPOSITE David's painting of the death of Jean-Paul Marat. As editor of *L'Ami du Peuple*, he was a popular spokesman of the revolutionary cause. Charlotte Corday made him a martyr to that cause when she stabbed him, and opened the way to further violence and extremism.

212

The note, which still survives, Michonis later made illegible by additional pinpricks. An expert claims to have deciphered these words: 'I am closely watched. I speak to no one. I trust you. I shall come.'

The plans went wrong when somehow Madame Richard got hold of the note and handed it over to Michonis. Since he was implicated in the plot, he pretended to treat the matter with no concern and advised her to say nothing of it. However, Gilbert now took fright and on 3 September reported the matter to his authorities. The night before there had been an abortive attempt to rescue the Queen from the Conciergerie. According to de Rougeville, he and Michonis went to the prison late that night, saying they had come to take Marie Antoinette back to the Temple, but in reality to take her to General Jarjayes's house outside Paris, before escaping to Germany. However, because of the threatening attitude of one *gendarme*, the whole scheme foundered.

Officials appointed by the Convention looked into the whole affair and, though they could prove nothing, this hastily conducted enquiry ended in the imprisonment of the Richards and a redoubled severity towards the Queen. Michonis, after having been kept a prisoner for three days in the Conciergerie, was incarcerated in the Abbaye on 8 September. Marie Antoinette had new jailers and her cell was thoroughly searched, the investigations going so far as to 'overturn the bed and the chairs'. They took from her, her two rings, confiscated her linen and left only her bonnets and fichus. Henceforth there was a particular ban on giving her flowers, and even the food was reduced to a minimum.

On 11 September, the day of the Richards' arrest, six police officers arrived at the Conciergerie 'to choose a place of detention for the widow Capet other than the one where she is at present detained'. The room now chosen had formerly been used as the pharmacy. Of the three openings which let in the daylight, two were blocked, one with a sheet of iron, the other by masonry, while the third was to be partially bricked up and covered by a strong and closely latticed grille. Her new jailers, the Baults, from the prison of La Force, were at first far less amenable than Monsieur and Madame Richard, for it had been made clear to them by the Commune that they were answerable with their lives for the Queen's person. But they too, in the following weeks, were humanized and were to become still more devoted and helpful than her former jailers.

She had been left with hardly anything. Even her linen had

214

been confiscated and she was now allowed only one chemise at a time at infrequent intervals, as instructed by the Revolutionary Tribunal. Rosalie would try to help by slipping her own under the Queen's bolster when she made her bed. She had even been refused candles and, as the days were getting shorter, the only light to enter her cell was from a lamp in the Cour des Femmes outside her half boarded-up window. 'I spun out as long as possible the various little preparations for the night', recalled the young girl, long afterwards, 'so that my revered mistress might not be left alone in the dark until the last possible minute.' At the beginning of October the nights were growing colder and damp lined the walls of the cell. 'She complained of it in her gentle way; and as for me, I was so upset because I could do nothing to make things easier for her. In the evenings I took her nightgown from under the bolster and ran up to my room to get it really hot at the fire. Then I put it back under the bolster along with the large fichu the Queen wore at night.' Under her feeble cotton covering the Queen would lie shivering. She had asked Bault for a woollen covering, but when Fouquier, the Public Prosecutor, heard of the request, he threatened the jailer with the guillotine. By now, the bad air and lack of exercise were fast undermining her health, and she now began to suffer acute attacks of internal haemorrhage.

The Carnation Plot, apart from condemning her to this stricter and more uncomfortable supervision, had a further result in that it hastened her trial and appearance before the Revolutionary Tribunal. For a long time, even after her removal to the Conciergerie, the leaders of the Revolution had by no means decided on her fate, and several members of the Convention had voted for the Queen's trial only as a means of coercing the Allies. Marie Antoinette, herself, still held out hope and Rosalie, long afterwards, said that on one occasion when the death of Louis XVI was referred to in the Queen's presence, she observed that 'He was fortunate in that he had died for France, but that she herself expected to be sent to Austria with her children.' The discovery of the plot, however, now gave the extremists their long-awaited chance to force the hands of the more timid among their colleagues.

For about a month fruitless attempts were made to find matter for the act of accusation, and even on 3 October, when the Convention decreed that the Revolutionary Tribunal 'shall deal immediately and uninterruptedly with the judgment', there were still no grounds for the trial. It was to be her eight-year-old son, brutalized and terrorized as he was by his keepers, who was to

let fall a compromising and slanderous reply to a question he could not understand. Marie Antoinette, as a result, was to be charged with having an incestuous relationship with her own son. Hébert, who went to see the little King in the Temple, fired questions at him and bullied him for the right answers. Both Daujon and Goret were present at the cross-examination.

The young prince [recorded Daujon] was sitting in an armchair, swinging his little legs for his feet did not reach the ground. He was examined about the statements in question and was asked if they were true: he answered affirmatively. At once Madame Elizabeth, who was present, cried out: 'Oh, the monster!' As for me [added Daujon], I could not consider this answer came from the child himself because of his air of uneasiness, and his whole manner made me feel it was a suggestion put to him by another person and that he may have been threatened with punishment or ill-treatment if he did not comply.

On 12 October, two hours after she had gone to bed, Marie Antoinette was woken and brought to the Grand' Chambre in the Palais de Justice. By the light of two candles she found herself facing Fouquier-Tinville, the Deputy Public Prosecutor, and Hermann, the President of the Revolutionary Tribunal. The old charges were revived once more: the millions despatched to Austria, the understanding with the *émigrés*, the treason of the so-called 'Austrian society', the plots to massacre the people. She replied to the accusations with calm and dignity, and Hermann presently grew tired of baiting the prisoner with no success. The preliminary investigation drew to a close with no mention made of the charge Hébert was preparing concerning herself and the ex-Dauphin.

Two advocates were now chosen to defend her: Chaveau-Lagarde and Tronson du Coudray. Her trial was to begin at eight o'clock on the morning of 14 October, a trial that was to last for two whole days and nights. All through those hours, the Queen, dressed in mourning, her hair covered by a white linen cap with a band of black crêpe, sat proudly confronting Fouquier-Tinville and listened unflinchingly to the prosecution, to the insulting questions put to her by the President and Jury and to the occasional threatening murmurs of the *tricoteuses* who were clustered together in the corner. Her hands alone betrayed her inward agitation, as her fingers drummed nervously on the bar in front of her. She heard again the charge of sending French gold to Austria, of causing foreign warfare and inciting civil strife. Then came Hébert's

OPPOSITE Kucharsky's unfinished portrait of Marie Antoinette in the last year of her life, her hair turned white through shock, and prematurely aged through suffering. But those who saw her at this time were still impressed by the Queen's beauty and serenity.

217

Marie Antoinette listens gravely while the accusations against her are read out in her cell. A contemporary engraving.

accusation. She heard herself described as being so perverted and so used to all crimes, 'that forgetting she was a mother and disregarding the limitations set by the laws of nature, she had not been afraid to practise with Louis Capet, her son, indecencies whose very idea and whose mere name arouse a shudder'. Even Madame Elisabeth's name was brought into the catalogue of indecencies as Hébert stood up to testify as a witness. Not for a moment did the Queen betray her feelings. 'I have no knowledge of the inci-

218

dents of which Hébert speaks,' was all she said, in a quiet voice. Later on in the proceedings, one of the jurors reminded her again that she had not answered what went on between herself and her son. Only then did she rise to her feet: 'If I did not answer it was because nature cannot answer such a charge brought against a mother.' She paused and then turned towards the spectators: 'I appeal to all mothers here!' For a moment there was silence and then such a commotion that there were calls for order. Hébert's accusation had badly misfired.

At the close of the second day's sitting nothing had been proved against the Queen. Public opinion was favourable and a workman was even overheard to say: 'She will get off. She spoke like an angel. They will only banish her.' Following her reply to the question of incest, she had whispered to Chaveau-Lagarde: 'Was there too much dignity in my answer?' And seeing his surprise, she added: 'Because I heard a woman of the people say to her neighbour: "How proud she is."' Perhaps she feared her judges would form the same opinion. By now she was physically exhausted. She had been ill for several weeks, and for twenty-four hours she had swallowed only a little soup and a glass of water, hardly enough to stop her from fainting. At midnight the case for the prosecution was over. Two hours later Chaveau-Lagarde sat down after making his defence and Marie Antoinette remarked gently to him that he must be very tired. Not long afterwards Fouquier-Tinville ordered his arrest, followed shortly by that of his colleague. It was then Hermann's turn to sum up. Cleverly, he never mentioned Hébert's charges, but concentrated on the Queen's political activities to the detriment of France before and after the outbreak of the Revolution. Though he could prove nothing, since the evidence for the most part was in letters to Mercy, many of the charges were unfortunately true.

It was not until three in the morning that the jury retired to consider their verdict. It was almost a foregone conclusion. The Queen was brought into the hall, and motionless and dry-eyed she heard the verdict of guilty. Fouquier-Tinville demanded the death penalty. She seemed, said Chaveau-Lagarde, 'more surprised than dismayed'. When asked if she had anything to say, she only shook her head and, opening the gate of the bar at which she stood, she walked out of the hall in silence. As she walked down the staircase, she was obliged to ask the help of de Busne, the officer of her guard: 'I can hardly see,' she said to him. A moment later she stumbled, but he managed to save her before she fell. Uncon-

One of the famous *tricoteuses* of the National Convention, always gruesomely present with their knitting to watch the heads fall from the guillotine. A contemporary drawing.

sciously, he held his hat in his hand as he escorted her.

It was nearly five in the morning when the Queen re-entered the Conciergerie, where she was put into the condemned cell. By the light of two candles she wrote her last letter, to Madame Elisabeth:

16 October, at half-past four in the morning. It is to you, my sister, that I am writing for the last time. I have just been sentenced to death, but not one that is shameful, for it is only shameful for criminals, and I am going to rejoin your brother. Innocent like him, I hope I shall exhibit the same firmness that he did in his last moments. . . . Goodbye, my good and loving sister. I hope this letter will reach you. Think of me always. I send you my deepest love, and also to my poor, dear children. Goodbye. Goodbye.

Blotted with tears, the letter still exists in the National Archives, but it was never to reach Madame Elisabeth for Fouquier-Tinville intercepted it before it could reach the Temple.

At seven o'clock, when Rosalie entered the cell, she found the Queen stretched out on her bed, staring up at the window, with her head resting on her hand. She was exhausted, both physically and emotionally. The servant girl had brought her some soup, but Marie Antoinette refused it: 'I shall never want anything more, my child. It is all over for me.' But Rosalie insisted and she reluctantly swallowed a few spoonfuls. An hour later she returned to help the Queen dress, sheltering her against the stare of the officer on guard who, even at this last moment, refused to look away. She put on a black petticoat and white skirt, a white bodice tied with ribbons at the wrist, and a white bonnet. Now there was nothing left for Rosalie to do. 'I left without daring to say a word of farewell or make even a curtsey, for I was afraid of compromising or upsetting her. I went to my room to cry and pray for her.' Soon afterwards a priest arrived who had taken the oath to the Constitution, but the Queen curtly refused to have anything to do with him and treated him as a complete stranger.

She was kneeling beside the bed when Larivière, the turnkey, came in. 'Larivière,' she said, 'you know they are going to kill me.' As she spoke, four members of the Tribunal came in, hat in hand, to read her the death sentence for the second time. 'It is unnecessary to read it. I know it only too well,' she said. 'No matter,' one of them replied, 'it must be read to you again.' A few minutes later, Henri Sanson, whose father had guillotined Louis, entered the cell. 'Hold out your hands,' he ordered her. For a moment the Queen drew back. 'Must my hands be bound?' she asked, 'Louis

Marie Antoinette before her judges: a contemporary engraving. Her composure in the face of monstrous charges won her the sympathy of the public present at the trial.

220

Portrait de Marie Antoinette Reine
de France conduite au Supplice, déssiné à la
plume par David, Spectateur du Convoi, et placé
à une fenêtre avec la citoyenne Tullien, épouse
du Représentant Tullien, de qui je tiens cette
pièce.
Copié sur l'original existant dans la Collection Soularie.

Further Reading

Original sources

Correspondence secrète entre Marie-Thérèse et le Comte de
    Mercy-Argenteau, ed. d'Arneth and A. Geffroy, 3 vols (Paris 1875)
Journal of Louis XVI, published by Louis Nicolardot (Paris 1873)
Private Memoirs by the Duchesse d'Angoulême (London 1817)
Memoirs of Madame Campan (London 1823)
Memoirs of Madame de Tourzel (Paris 1883)

Other works

Nolhac, P. de, *Marie Antoinette Dauphine* (Paris 1898)
    La Reine Marie-Antoinette (London 1905)
    Le Trianon de Marie Antoinette (London 1925)
Lenôtre, G., *The Flight of Marie Antoinette* (London 1906)
    The Last Days of Marie Antoinette (London 1907)
Belloc, Hilaire, *Marie Antoinette* (London 1910)
Heidenstamm, O. -g. de, *The Letters of Marie Antoinette, Fersen and*
    Barnave (London 1926)
Zweig, Stefan, *Marie Antoinette* (London 1933)
Webster, N. H., *Louis XVI and Marie Antoinette* (London 1936)
Castelot, André, *Marie Antoinette* (Paris 1953)
Cobban, A., *History of Modern France*, vol. I (London 1962)
Mayer, Dorothy Moulton, *Marie Antoinette: The Tragic Queen*
    (London 1968)
Furneaux, Rupert, *The Bourbon Tragedy* (London 1968)
Huisman, Philippe, and Jallut, Marguerite, *Marie Antoinette*
    (London 1971)
Fersen, Axel von, *Rescue the Queen: a Diary of the French Revolution*
    1789–93 (London 1971)
Hearsey, John, *Marie Antoinette* (London 1972)
Loomis, Stanley, *The Fatal Friendship* (London 1972)

The House of Bourbon

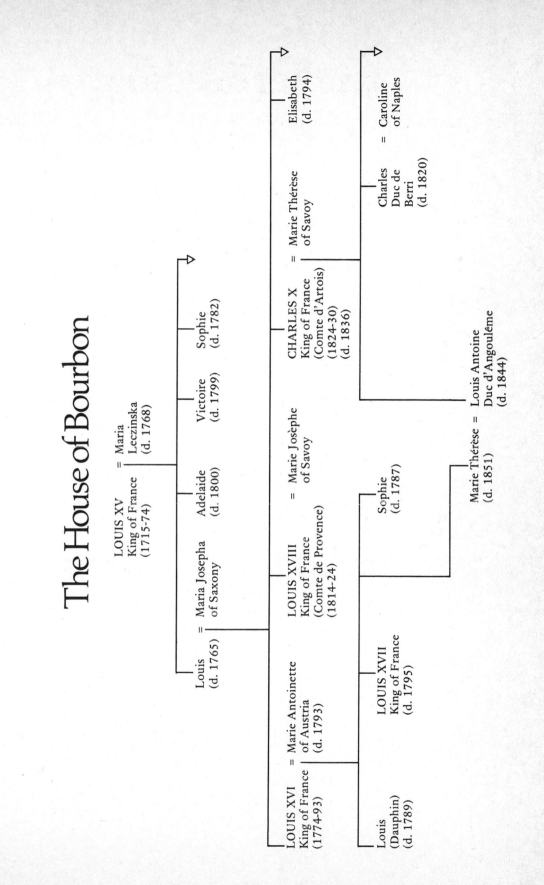

List of Illustrations

226

Picture research by Pat Hodgson.
Maps and family tree drawn by Design Practitioners Limited.

Index

231